Listen for

GOD Whispers

Liz Thompson

Nudges, Fudges and Butterfly Moments

Liz Thompson

Jebaire Publishing, LLC
Snellville, GA 30078

God Whispers
Copyright©2012 Liz Thompson
Published by Jebaire Publishing, LLC

All rights reserved. No part of this publication may be reproduced or transmitted in any form or by any means, electronic or mechanical, including photocopying and recording, or by any information storage and retrieval system, without written permission from the author.

All scripture quotations, unless otherwise indicated, are taken from the Holy Bible, New International Version®, NIV®. Copyright ©1973, 1978, 1984, 2011 by Biblica, Inc.™ Used by permission of Zondervan. All rights reserved worldwide. www.zondervan.com The "NIV" and "New International Version" are trademarks registered in the United States Patent and Trademark Office by Biblica, Inc.™ Used by permission. All rights reserved. Scripture marked (NASB) are taken from the New American Standard Bible © 1960, 1962, 1963, 1968, 1971, 1972, 1973, 1977, by the Lockman Foundation. Used by permission. (ISBN 0-87981-912-X). Scripture marked (NLT) are taken from the Holy Bible, New Living Translation © 1996. Used by permission of Tyndale House Publications Inc., Wheaton, Illinois, 60189. All rights reserved. ISBN 0-8423-3425-4.

ISBN-13: 978-0-9838548-5-2
Library of Congress Control Number: 2012947898

Interior Editor: Renee Cooper
Supervising Editor: Shannon Clark
Cover Design: Jebaire Publishing, LLC

Visit Liz Thompson at:
www.lizthompsonbooks.com

Visit Jebaire's website at:
www.jebairepublishing.com

DEDICATION

This book is dedicated to the Great Shepherd who has guided me throughout my life. He is also the Great Weaver of my life for which I am eternally grateful that He sees the upper side of my life's tapestry.

TABLE OF CONTENTS

Foreword / 7

Acknowledgments / 9

Introduction / 11

Butterfly Moments / 16

Nudges / 21

Fudges / 45

This Little Light of Mine / 59

Jesus Our Shepherd / 83

Warts and All, He Still Loves Us / 87

Crazy Quilt of a Life / 97

Raise Up Your Voice / 104

God's Word For Us / 108

Only God Can Make a Tree / 134

Inconvenience or Opportunity? / 154

The Good News / 161

Appendix 1: Suggested Reading and Websites /165

Appendix 2: Contributor Biographies / 166

Appendix 3: Fudge Recipes / 172

Appendix 4: Quote References / 176

Appendix 5: Music Notes (pun intended) / 181

FOREWORD

I love the way God keeps His promise in Romans 8:28 and makes everything work out for the good of those who love Him. He has His hands full with most of us; we make more than our fair share of mistakes. We do our best to ignore His nudges at times, but, thank God, He is persistent and consistent. I am reminded every day that God said, "My grace is sufficient for you" (2 Corinthians 12:9). I love the assurance that comes with that promise. Like the Apostle Paul, we can all shout, "By the grace of God I am what I am, and his grace to me was not without effect" (1 Corinthians 15:10). On the contrary, it has had a tremendous effect!

Having been a pastor for more than twenty-five years, I have learned to place a high value on those moments when God has nudged His way and His will firmly into my heart. In fact, the strongest "nudges" often come in the middle of or immediately following my efforts to "fudge."

I remember one of my fudges, in particular. I was absolutely certain in 1994 that God wanted me to go somewhere and plant a church from scratch. I had accepted an interim ministry at a small, struggling church thirty minutes from my home. They had asked that I make it permanent, but I kept telling them no. I interviewed with three different church planting organizations over a seven-month period. Each time it looked like a go for me, but each time God closed the door. Finally, I was invited to a meeting a state a way. The director of this group told me it was just a formality. I drove through a hammering snowstorm to get there. When I returned home the next night, I called the director, and he told me that they were quite sure I was the man for the job—until a minister on the hiring team decided he wanted the job. Just like that, I was out, and he was in.

Suddenly, I realized that I was being "nudged" in a different direction. For seven months, I had been trying to "fudge" my way out of God's will while God was trying to "nudge" me to stay in it. As I write this foreword, I am in my seventeenth year in that small church. There have been some big struggles along the way, but I am happy to say that I am glad I finally let God "nudge" me away from my "fudge."

I am confident that you have similar stories, some with happy endings and others with "not so happy" endings. No matter how they ended, they are all a part of your story. It is your story and no one else's. While few, if any, of us can be proud of everything we have done in the past, we can be sure that there is a purpose for all the nudges and fudges along the way. And we can certainly know that the "butterfly moments" have and will continue to come. The key is to watch and listen for God's whisper. Liz Thompson wrote this book so that we can go through life with our eyes and hearts wide open and notice how God uses nudges, fudges, and butterfly moments to help us remember that He is God and we are not!

Stan Kirtlan[1]
Pastor
Buckeye Christian Church
Grove City, Ohio

---

1   See Appendix: Contributor Biographies

ACKNOWLEDGMENTS

Anyone who has written a book knows that it happens on countless levels and with the help of many people. Although this book was inspired by my life's nudges, fudges and butterfly moments, God sent people into this writing process to fill the pages with their meaningful experiences and work, so it's not all about me.

The contributors are as diverse as life itself. Thank you for your patience during the editing and publishing process. I've been blessed with new friendships and forged deeper ones throughout this book's journey to publication, and I know that others will be blessed by your willingness to share your experiences. I encourage each of you to continue writing.

For those who offered loved ones' writings posthumously, please know that I am grateful. My hope is that this book honors their memory and continues their legacy and love for the Lord.

My nudge to write is strong most days and my husband's patience in this never ceases to amaze me. He remains the love of my life and sharing our daily lives together is a blessing.

May God bless each of you as you read on.

INTRODUCTION

God desires and is pleased to communicate with us through the avenues of our minds, our wills, and our emotions. The continuous and unembarrassed interchange of love and thought between God and the souls of the redeemed men and women is the throbbing heart of the New Testament.
—A. W. Tozer[2]

Where are you at this moment? If your first reaction was to say, "I am in a book store," or "I am in my recliner", I would likely say the same thing. But what I am asking is where you are in your faith walk with God. Do you feel far from Him? Maybe you walk closely with Him and hear His voice in your life. Are you in a listening mode or are you tuned into the "noise" in your life, cluttered with things to do, places to go, and people to see?

Maybe you picked up this book because you were curious how God could possibly whisper. Or maybe you needed to make a major decision and you thought this book might help. Or maybe you picked it up because when you saw "fudge" in the subtitle, you thought it might be a recipe book. It is a recipe book, in its own way, and for fun, you will find fudge recipes in the appendix. But I wrote this book to share some experiences of mine, and those of its contributors, about how we learned from our fudges and responded to God's nudges. God wants to free us from our self-made cocoons, or chrysalises, and watch us fly free like a butterfly.

The Webster Dictionary definition may help you catch my mean-

[2] See Appendix: Quote References

Introduction

ing. Nudge: "…to touch or push gently; to seek the attention of by a push of the elbow; to prod lightly: urge into action"[3] Can you see how God would use nudges to get our attention in this definition?

Most people understand fudge as a candy, but there is a deeper meaning to the word. Fudge means both chocolate candy and "To devise as a substitute; to fail to come to grips with; to exceed the proper bounds or limits of; to fail to perform as expected: to avoid commitment.

Example: The treasurer fudged the figures."[4]

When I to fail to have no time to shop for what I need, I fudge my way through hoping for the best. When God nudges us, we might ignore Him or think we heard wrong. We may do nothing or only part of what He asks and regret it later. This is my definition of fudging in this book.

Butterfly Moments is my favorite part of the title. It means we are freed, liberated by God to live the life He has planned for us. We shed the old wrappings of our life, see more clearly, love more dearly, and follow Jesus more nearly than before. Sound familiar? Those are the key words of the song "Day by Day" from the musical Godspell.

We begin to grow from baby Christians, where we all begin, to mature Christians who have an unquenchable desire to know and understand more.

In this book, you will read stories of people who responded to God's nudges, some who also fudged their response, and butterfly moments when we feel free. My hope is you will be able to relate, be encouraged, and remember your own experiences, and the next time you think God is nudging you, you will recognize it and act accordingly. Forgiveness is abundant from God. "Therefore, my friends, I want you to know that through Jesus the forgiveness of sins is proclaimed to you" (Acts 13:38).

I'll begin with the last part of the subtitle because that's the Good News! Sharing good news at the beginning of a conversation is wise, in "my book" and will allow you to move on to wherever God leads you.

May our Lord Jesus Christ himself and God our Father, who loved us and by his grace gave us eternal encouragement and good hope, encourage your hearts and strengthen you in every good deed and word.
-2 Thessalonians 2:16-17

---

[3] http://www.merriam-webster.com/dictionary/nudge
[4] http://www.merriam-webster.com/dictionary/fudge

Disturb Me
**Ben Cachiaras[5], 2010 NACC President
(North American Christian Convention)**

Dear God, disturb me.
Rouse me from sleepy paths of comfortable faith
That too easily become dangerous ruts of safety
Rather than the adventurous path
You have called me to walk with you.
Forgive me for focusing more
On what I want you to do for "my ministry" and "my life"
Than what you may want me to do
For you and for your kingdom.
Help me to remember that your call to me
Is simply to follow --
And that you are on the move
Always.
Push me, Jesus, with the lifting power of your Spirit
Out of stagnant places I've been in
Prod me past the horizons formed by my fear
Give me an attitude that is finally ready to follow you, Jesus
No matter what.
I want to go beyond.
I really do, Lord.
Where you lead me, I will follow.
No turning back.
Amen.

Therefore, as God's chosen people, holy and dearly loved, clothe yourselves with compassion, kindness, humility, gentleness and patience. Bear with each other and forgive whatever grievances you may have against one another. Forgive as the Lord forgave you. And over all these virtues put on love, which binds them all together in perfect unity.

Let the peace of Christ rule in your hearts, since as members of one body you were called to peace. And be thankful. Let the message of Christ dwell among you richly as you teach and admonish one another with all wisdom through psalms, hymns, and songs from the Spirit, singing to God with grati-

---

5   Appendix Contributor Biographies

tude in your hearts. And whatever you do, whether in word or deed, do it all in the name of the Lord Jesus, giving thanks to God the Father through him.
Colossians 3:12-17

He Sends His Love (Lyrics)
(Liz Thompson, 1993)

>He took my hand and led the way
>He led the way for I could not see;
>He called my name with His quiet voice
>Even though I could not hear.
>He touched my heart though I could not feel.
>He sent me love on angel's wings;
>His patience makes my heart rejoice
>For now I hear His voice!
>
>Reach out your hand and close your eyes
>Let the world go by – go ahead and cry.
>Hear His loving voice – He sings to you
>Hear the song God sings – then you can rejoice.
>He will never leave – He is always near
>He loves you even though you move away.
>He will call to you in a special way;
>So you'll walk right to His arms.
>
>Chorus:
>Maybe in a song or a silent time
>In a sleepless night or a baby's smile
>In the springtime air or the winter snow
>All we need to know is God is everywhere
>(last time: God is always near)
>Maybe in a song or a silent prayer
>
>He sends His love on angel's wings.

The voices of the world are loud and sparse, but the voice of God is a constant whisper.

-Benjamin J. Elger[6]

---

6   See Appendix: Quote References

1

Butterfly Moments

Joy is the experience of knowing that you are unconditionally loved.
-Henri Nouwen (1921-1996)[7]

Then you will know the truth, and the truth will set you free.
-John 8:32

    A movement caught my eye. Was it a reflection from the sun? Unsure, I moved in the direction it came from and found a rusty lantern we'd taken down last winter and hadn't thrown away. Once the snow melted, all kinds of finds were appearing on our patio.
    I jumped when I picked up the rusty thing. Inside was a trapped butterfly, blue and beautiful, caught in the small space with no exit. Since the small door was rusted, I called to Bob, my husband, who was out front cleaning the yard.
    "Bob, there's a butterfly trapped in here, and I can't get the door open."
    He took it gently and pried the door open with some tool he had in the garage. The butterfly struggled to move out of the opening and finally was free.
    It fell to the ground, and Bob reached for it. "His wing's bent," he told me.
    I almost cried but took it in my hand.
    "I'll go out back with it and see if it will calm down enough to fly," I said.
    I grabbed my camera on my way through the kitchen to the

---

7   See Appendix: Quote References

patio, hoping I would catch a shot of this beauty. Outside, it finally settled on my denim-clad leg and fluttered its wings or, rather, wing. Talking to it, I prayed it would live long enough to enjoy the breezy spring day. After I took a few photos, I carried the butterfly to the back of our yard where we have Shasta daisies growing. I placed it on one of the blooms and shot a few more pictures.

The song "His Eye is on the Sparrow" came to mind. I knew God made everything and seeing the injury to this small creature, I guessed it was not long for this earth. Leaving it to sun itself, I walked to our garden to do some work.

Later, Bob told me that the cocoon[8] was in the lantern, and of course, I took a photo of that as well.

Later that evening, Bob told me he found the butterfly on the ground, dead. We knew this was going to happen, but we were a little sad anyway. It was a reminder of how delicate and short life is for every living thing.

Butterflies fascinate me with their beauty and delicate nature. Jokingly, I have called them Flutterbys. While I was a reporter for *Suburban News Publications* (SNP) in Columbus, Ohio, I had what I called a Butterfly Moment.

Since that time, it has become clear to me that I was being nudged gently by God and my eyes and heart were being opened to life as I'd never seen it before that day. It was a freeing moment and a theme that will repeat throughout this book.

Butterfly Moments Can Come at Any Age [9]
(Liz Thompson)

I know how a butterfly must feel when it breaks out of its cocoon and spreads its wings. I must have been eight or nine years old when a Monarch butterfly landed on my tennis shoe and slowly spread its wings, showing its vibrant colors. Fully expecting it to take flight, I held my breath. It stayed on my shoe. I remember looking around so I could find someone to share the moment with, but I was the sole witness of what I considered miraculous. I doubt the word miraculous popped into my young brain. More likely it was something like "special" or "wow" that occurred to me.

So special was this moment that some forty years later I can still remember I was in the alley between the Minors' and the Bagleys' homes. Houses took on the name and personalities of the owners in

---

8   The butterfly really breaks out of a chrysalis, but most people call it a cocoon.
9   Printed in SNP June 6, 2001.

Old Westerville in the '50s. At least, to me, they did. I stood watching the butterfly, wondering what it meant that it stayed on my shoe so long. Did the butterfly like me? Had it chosen me? Remember, I was young. Time passed slowly on that hot summer day, and I didn't move for fear the butterfly would take flight. Enjoying the company, I remember talking to it. People who know me realize it doesn't take much for me to begin talking.

Of course, eventually, it did fly away, and I pedaled my lavender and blue bicycle, that my Dad had put together for me from old bike parts, home as fast as I could. I ran into our old house yelling for my Mom, so I could share my butterfly experience with her. I think it was difficult for her to tell me that the butterfly had just freed itself from a cocoon and only paused to dry its wings, but I knew it had chosen me to share its special moment of freedom.

Often we spend a lifetime binding ourselves into a self-made cocoon. I am not sure why this is often a human condition. We look, speak, and act as society dictates, often losing our sense of self and thus losing true freedom. Thoughts occur to me at what might seem like odd times—in the car driving, in the shower, and in dreams. Those all are times when I cannot act on the idea without great inconvenience.

While driving to interview a man running for public office, I had my butterfly moment. Thinking about my work, I understood how a butterfly must feel when it sheds its cocoon and spreads its wings while flying to freedom. It was a profound thought for me because I realized I felt that same freedom. I felt unbound and finally free to love life unabashedly and do what I love to do: meet people and write. "Wow!" entered my mind just as it had when that monarch butterfly landed on my shoe many years ago.

After that interview was complete, I dared to share my new thought with this man I had just met. It seemed appropriate, and inside I chuckled when his response was "Wow." He and I talked about our shared goal of wanting to make a difference in this world. Our discussion was injected with new energy when we talked about representing people honestly and well. Integrity. Values. Freedom. These are not new thoughts or ideas. But when you experience them in a way that reaches into your soul, it is all new and fresh. Everything I experience has taken on a new vitality as if I had been partially asleep and now am awakened. I didn't realize how uninformed and uninvolved I had been prior to the last six months as a reporter.

I had no regrets and was thankful that, as I turned a half-century old, I could begin with an awareness that had been hidden as I was in my cocoon. Without the life experiences of the last fifty years, I most likely would never have shed that old cocoon, dried my wings, and taken flight. Plus, with experience, fears of change and of learning are gone.

So I am running into my old house to share my news with you.

> ***It is for freedom that Christ has set us free. Stand firm, then, and do not let yourselves be burdened again by a yoke of slavery.***
> ***Galatians 5:1***

In late May of 2010, our ten-year-old grandson, Andrew, called me on the phone.

"Nana, I have something to tell you!" The excitement in his voice let me know it was good news.

"I found a caterpillar yesterday and put it in a jar. And guess what?"

I told him I didn't know.

"This morning the caterpillar is in a cocoon!"

"Wow! That's wonderful, Andrew! That must have been exciting to see!" I said.

"It means it will become a butterfly, Nana!"

Then he shared something that reminded me of the way I think.

"Nana, it's really strange because the night before I thought, 'Wouldn't it be neat if it became a butterfly?' and now it will be!"

A few days later, I heard from him again with another excited conversation. He had found a number of caterpillars, and they were all in cocoons. When I saw him next, he had the jar in his hand. He didn't say anything to me, but I knew he wanted to show me. It was interesting that the multiple cocoons were all in one corner of the jar like a white mass of cotton candy without the pink or blue colors. It was a joy to share in his excitement all over again.

Years ago, my daughter, Mary, Andrew's mom, bought a butterfly hatching kit for the children, Jacob, Elizabeth, and Andrew. They watched the cocoons until the butterflies broke free and it was time to set the butterflies free. After watching them flutter away into the air, Andrew cried and hoped they would return to them. For days, they watched for signs of their beloved butterflies, only to be saddened each time they realized they were truly gone from the gentle grasp of their tiny hands.

That is how parents feel when their children "break free" from their home and fly free as adults. Even as I write those words, tears are on the edge of my eyes when I remember watching them go out on their own. I wasn't quite prepared for the tears I cried when they left, but I knew it was time for them to go.

Smoky Mountain Butterflies

Flying free, like a butterfly, is truly freeing– and brings believers together. We gravitate toward others who believe in Christ. A perfect example happened in May of 2010 as we were setting up camp in the Great Smoky Mountains outside of Gatlinburg, Tennessee.

As we drove into the park, we noticed hundreds of yellow butterflies flying everywhere, or so it seemed. Once we parked in our campsite, I walked around our car to watch some of these beauties.

What I saw made me grab my camera. Butterflies were darting up and down over a spot of leaves on the ground. I moved closer and saw about twenty of them fluttering their wings in a type of huddle. A few would fly up, and more would come down. It was amazing to see, but I wondered why they were bunched together like that.

After I snapped a few photos, our daughter and her family arrived at their campsite next to us. I called them over quickly to see the butterflies. We hugged briefly before I moved them over to see the sight of the butterflies. Our grandchildren, Jake, Beth, and Andrew stood there with their mouths open, yet smiling. There was one blue butterfly fluttering just outside the bunch of yellow ones.

A couple walking by saw the butterflies, stopped, and took out their camera. We talked about seeing all the butterflies in the park. They snapped some photos and were on their way. Soon after, a volunteer for the park stopped by and I asked him what he thought the occasion was for the flock of butterflies to be congregated in such a way.

"They do that to get warm," he said. "They are attracted to bear or other animal dung to get warm."

Not an attractive thought, but it made sense.

I was so glad we had seen this because, the next day, and the following four days, we only saw occasional butterflies in the campsite.

As Christians, we huddle like these butterflies. Whom do you think the blue butterfly represents? My first thought was a non-Christian looking on. Then I settled on the idea that the blue butterfly represents Jesus. He was looking on the others as a shepherd watches over his sheep. That's my story and I'm sticking with it!

When you come to the end of all the light you know, and it's time to step into the darkness of the unknown, faith is knowing that one of two things will happen: Either you will be given something solid to stand on or you will be taught to fly.
-Edward Teller[10]

---

10   See Appendix: Quote References

2

Nudges

You also must be ready, because the Son of Man will come at an hour when you do not expect him.
-Luke 12:40

SURPRISE VISITS

God has surprised me oodles of times in my life even literally waking me up many a night. Looking back, I realize these were visits and blessings from God Himself, though, at the time, I was frustrated that I could not sleep.

Night Peace
(Liz Thompson)

>Sometimes I lay awake at night
>Wondering what to do.
>Replaying the last day I spent
>Living the day through.
>My mind does not want to rest
>I desire to, with sleep, be blessed.
>Rather, lay awake I do.
>Hours later, off I drift
>To slumber, dreams new.
>Waking, I hope to feel at rest, and usually I do.
>Is God attempting to stir my soul,
>And I roll over and ignore?
>When I lay awake at night

And arise to take pen in hand,
The words that flow steadily from my heart
Often help me understand,
Pleased I listened to His gentle nudge,
Feeling blessed and full of love.
For I think God stirs us up,
Makes us think, and wakes us up.
Yet we think we just cannot sleep,
Tossing and turning, wanting night's peace.
If we submit our lives to God,
In the restless hours at night,
He will stir our souls a bit.
So have a candle and keep it lit,
And when we finally go to sleep,
Angels will soothe us and rest will be deep.

You may remember the TV show *Candid Camera* where Allen Funt would film people doing everyday things in unusual circumstances. The theme song was catchy, saying, "When you least expect it, you're elected, it's your lucky day. Smile! You're on Candid Camera." Being nudged by God has nothing to do with luck, but it really is typically when we "least expect it." Despite the fact that we have no idea when God might nudge us, we must always be ready. We need to see Jesus in every moment of our life. Jesus surrounded himself with children whenever possible when He was on earth; therefore the simplicity and uncluttered mind of a child is precious to God. He wants all of us to have the wonder of a child and believe that God will talk to us. If we want God to use us, we need to take care our lives are not so busy that we won't be able to hear or feel God instructing us.

God is looking for those with whom He can do the impossible—what a pity that we plan only the things that we can do by ourselves.
-A. W. Tozer[11]

A Voice?

Whether you turn to the right or to the left, your ears will hear a voice behind you, saying, "This is the way; walk in it."
Isaiah 30:21

---

11   See Appendix: Quote References

Do you hear it? Do you sense something? You shake your head, thinking you are hearing things. No one is in the room with you, yet you heard a voice whispering. What did the voice say? You repeat it aloud to wrap your mind around the words. You don't understand.

This might be a message from God to do something. My experience has been that I suddenly know or sense I'm to do or say something. It might be to talk to that person standing over by the table alone, give that dollar to the homeless person, hug that friend you love, call that friend you miss, write that poem, song, or story, share that embarrassing experience you are holding onto without forgiving yourself, seek forgiveness, or show forgiveness. If no harm would come from the action, I have learned that it is usually from God. We won't always know the result, but we will know we followed through.

It's not about us.

Most often, my experience is that I never know the result of following through with a nudge. A clear example of this happened to me on a weekday in the late summer of 2010. I had several books due to be returned to the local library. I love the library and always have. In our little burg of Grove City, Ohio, the library is about three-quarters of a mile from our home.

It was a beautiful summer day, promising to be cooler than the continual ninety-degree weather we'd been having. I was sitting on our patio thinking on my day when clearly I heard, "Go to the library." I actually argued that I had housework to do and that the library books were not overdue. I heard it again, "Go to the library. Now." I looked at my dog, Toby, and said, "I guess we'd better get ready to go to the library!" His ears perked up, knowing he was getting a walk. I put on my shoes, gathered my books and purse, latched Toby's leash on his harness, and off we went, me in my power wheelchair (due to a combination of common sense and my multiple sclerosis, I have not driven a car since 2004) and Toby jogging beside me.

About five minutes into the trip, I realized I had forgotten my cell phone which I always had for emergencies. Though tempted to return home, I felt another nudge to keep going. So I did. Then I realized, for some reason I cannot remember, that I didn't have my library card. I quickly said my card number and thought, "OK, I don't need the card either." Toby and I kept moving.

Wondering all the way what God's plan for this quick trip was, I waited to see whom I might talk to or see that would give me a clue. I saw a few people, but no earth-shaking conversations or situations arose. I returned my books, picked up the ones I had on hold, surveyed a few shelves for other books I might want, and then left.

All the way home I kept thinking, "I wonder what this was all about?" Toby and I arrived home about an hour after we had left and went about our day.

That Sunday, I taught our women's Sunday school class, and the topic was grace. First, I had everyone sing the first two verses of Amazing Grace while I signed it in American Sign Language. We proceeded with the class, and at the end, I told about my not-so-profound trip to the library. As I talked, I realized I wouldn't know the outcome of that nudge from God and that was fine with me. Maybe someone smiled when they saw me rolling along with my dog in tow, and maybe that was the only smile they had found that day. On the other hand, maybe someone who needed to use a wheelchair saw me and discovered it might not be so bad after all. I will never know, and as I told the women my tale, I realized it was almost better this way because God knew what He was doing and I followed through. A minor thought came later that God may have been protecting us by removing us from our home for that hour. Although no danger seemed imminent before or after, it is a remote possibility.

Nudges come in many forms because God will reach us where we are and in a way we will understand. In theory, "What works for you may not work for me" seems true. Since God created us and has a purpose for us, it makes sense He would be giving us direction, as any loving father would do. Of course, a loving father also disciplines his children, so they will learn to fly and not crash.

You might not actually hear a voice but sense it knowing something is different in you to the point that you feel physically hot or cold, get chills, or wake up from a deep sleep just knowing. You may be driving and, without a thought, turn the wheel to go left instead of right. The gentle push God has given you may be to ensure you are in the right place at the right time for whatever God has in mind for you that day.

Different nudges come in forms of voices, praise, words of encouragement from others, scripture, ideas, beauty, music, poetry or prose, or silence..

Have you experienced it? Think about a time something unusual happened and afterwards you wondered how it came about, how you knew God had wanted you there at that moment to witness something, share, learn something, or help.

God uses us as His messengers to fulfill His plan.

Nudges

For we are God's handiwork, created in Christ Jesus to do good works, which God prepared in advance for us to do.
-Ephesians 2:10

For I know the plans I have for you (declares the LORD) plans to prosper you and not to harm you, plans to give you hope and a future.
-Jeremiah 29:11

Imagine. God prepared works in advance for us to do. He has plans for each of us. Look at the word "handiwork" in Ephesians 2:10. The Merriam-Webster Dictionary defines handiwork as work done by the hands or work done personally. The same definition gives this sentence as an example: "They admired the potter's beautiful *handiwork*," which flows into the next thought. By definition it means, "artistry; skillfulness; manner of execution." God as our creator has blessed us with his handiwork, has He not? This cannot be disputed when you look at the beauty of nature and the intricacies in each form of creation. We are God's creation. This verse says we are God's workmanship, which means we are His work of art. In essence, we are clay that God is molding and shaping every step of the way, reaching our unique core to do His work in us.

Yet you, LORD, are our Father. We are the clay, you are our potter; we are all the work of your hand.
-Isaiah 64:8

This verse makes me think of the hymn, "Have Thine Own Way Lord." Here is the first verse:

Have Thine own way, Lord! Have Thine own way!
Thou art the Potter, I am the clay.
Mold me and make me after Thy will,
While I am waiting, yielded and still. [12]

As God's children, we should want to do His work to please Him. Then the work will not be laborious but joyful.

God planned all our life experiences before we were born. This is a miraculous thought, and one that encourages me to keep doing what God wants me to do with my life and to keep listening for His direction, no matter what form it takes. *Amazing grace.*

---

12 See Appendix Music Notes

Finding others who have experienced God's nudges was inspiring. May you be blessed as you read these stories.

**Turn Left
(Kathleen Grimm Welty[13])**

It wasn't like a loud speaker or like a miniature angel sitting on my shoulder and speaking into my ear, out-shouting the red devil figure on the other side. And it wasn't like self-talk either. It was a voice from beyond me. It was the voice of God.

I was at the YMCA where my husband worked. This particular day was sunny and warm–the kind of day that makes kids want to run and play.

My husband and I were talking when a fellow employee rushed up to us with terror-filled eyes. She clung to her baby daughter as she explained her predicament.

She had been on her way to the parking lot after work and had gone out the door with her children, but she forgot something inside. Her five-year-old twin boys had begged her to stay outside in the big front yard while she took their baby sister and went back in. Besides begging, of course, they promised to stay in sight of the front door. Now, they were gone.

Everyone who had gathered in response to her frantic report wanted to help, terrified for her. We instinctively moved outside to watch while we planned what to do next. Within moments, we saw a wee figure approaching. It was one of the twins—alone. The mom handed her daughter to me, ran to her son, and scooped him into her arms; then he confessed their plan to walk home. He was sobbing and couldn't remember where he was when he left his brother or which path they took when they left.

We decided to fan out and search. It was before cell phones, so each of us established a certain search area. Two or three of us jumped into our cars to drive the perimeter, and several began to scour the neighborhood on foot.

Hopping into my car, I drove slowly. Nothing. I drove by their house on one corner and saw an alley running the length of their property. I drove down that alley at a snail's pace. Nothing. I drove around a few more blocks. Nothing. Then I thought up a plan to try one street further away from the "Y."

I ended up back at the same intersection, and this time I went

---

13   See Appendix Contributor Biographies

straight to carry out my further search. The light turned green, and immediately, at the exact time I needed to hear it, a voice said, "Turn left here, and go back to their house." I remember those exact words.

When I heard the Voice, I was compelled to turn left. I don't remember if I even had time to signal. I only remember the hard left turn of the tires and my calm obedience.

But their front porch was still empty! I turned, drove beside the house, and down the alley. Nothing. I stopped and stared at the back door. I was certain I should be noticing something. The Voice had been commanding and specific.

I squinted. I was ready to activate my emergency flashers when I saw a movement in the bushes. A red-eyed sobbing boy emerged from the greenery.

He stumbled toward me, a friendly face he longed for, but the tears continued. He huddled next to me as I drove, in record time, to the YMCA with my car horn blaring.

His mom thanked me over and over, but I told her it wasn't me she should thank. I obeyed a command of God. I had just spun the steering wheel. Left.

Impulsive or Responsive?
(Donna Lee Schillinger[14])

My daughter and I were on our way home from Devil's Den State Park, taking the scenic route through the mountains, when we stopped for lunch at a restaurant in the middle of nowhere. As we waited for our meal, I walked around the otherwise deserted dining area, and my gaze fixed on a flyer attached to a bulletin board, announcing a fundraiser at the restaurant the next Saturday. The announcement was cryptic. I couldn't figure out why the funds were needed, so when the waitress brought our food to us, I asked her for more information.

She told me that the funds would go to a couple who needed to pay off a large bill for an emergency air evacuation. About two weeks earlier, the man laid down with his 18-month old daughter to take a nap. When he woke up, his daughter wasn't there. She had woken up, gone to the door, opened it, and ventured down the driveway and to the road. Her father found her lying in the grass, barely alive. She was air evacuated but arrived dead at the hospital.

The parents had no idea what had happened though it was

---

14   See Appendix Contributor Biographies

obvious she had been hit by a vehicle. Then, a few days later, a man turned himself in. He admitted that he and a girlfriend had been joyriding down the highway while he was drunk. He saw the child too late and hit her accidentally, but without even slowing down, he drove off. When he sobered up, his conscience got the better of him, and he turned himself in even though there was a warrant for his arrest.

This kind of story is never easy to hear, but for me, it was excruciating. I was still grieving the recent passing of my own baby. I ate my lunch with a lump in my throat, and before I left, a still, small voice told me to make a contribution to this fundraiser. I wrote out a check (I can't recall for how much, but at least several hundred dollars), and with it, I wrote a note on a napkin. Again, I don't recall exactly what it said, but God gave me a message of comfort for that family. I gave it to the waitress and told her to please add it to the restaurant's fundraiser.

About a week later, I got a card in the mail from the mother. It said, "Donna, when still in pain from your loss, you reached out to us. I will never forget your kind words and expression of comfort. Knowing that in this world there are people like you makes me feel better. I will carry your hand-written note with me, to comfort me. So thank you for being there when this stranger needed you. Love, Diane."

The card bore the verse in I Thessalonians 5:11, saying, "So encourage each other and give each other strength just as you are now doing." Obviously, Diane's card encouraged me as well because I have kept it now for five years.

After I left the restaurant that day, I felt that maybe I had been impulsive leaving a large donation for a total stranger. But when I saw how God used the note and gift, I understood that I had not been impulsive, but rather responsive to that still, small voice.

Typically, we go about our daily routine considering our lives to be ordinary, commonplace, and without surprises and we can all relate to the following story because of that reality. . When God surprises us with an inspiration in our everyday lives, it bowls us over, and we may react just as this Rosemary did.

It is in the ordinary duties and labors of life that the Christian can and should develop his spiritual union with God.
-Thomas Merton[15]

---

15   See Appendix: Quote References

An Ordinary Day
(Rosemary Barkes[16])

It was an ordinary morning, an ordinary cup of coffee. I was wearing my ordinary robe, sitting at an ordinary table. Little did I know that something extraordinary was about to happen.

I sipped my steaming cup of brew and began to study the day's lesson from *The Upper Room*, a small pamphlet with daily readings published by the Methodist Church. The words jumped off the page—attacking me like a swarm of bees. The lesson was "From Brokenness to Blessing;" the gist of which was "Before we can be used greatly, we may have to be wounded deeply." Up until that moment, I had been carrying around excess baggage from a painful childhood. My entire body tingled with an unnerving yet soothing sensation. It was as if I were wrapped in a warm and fuzzy blanket.

The emotions rendered me helpless. I could do nothing but lower my head and weep. As I wept, I felt a slight pressure on my left shoulder, as if a friend were standing nearby offering a friendly hand to comfort me. But who? It couldn't have been my son. He was asleep on the living room sofa.

I began to sob uncontrollably. Amidst it all, I heard a voice whisper, "You have suffered enough; now go and put your talents to good use." Feeling totally powerless, I wondered, "Is this for real. What is going on?" Not having time to give it more thought, I grabbed a handful of tissues, wiped my eyes and nose, and stood up. Weak in the knees, I hustled to get my son ready for school and myself to the office.

By the time I got to work, I was feeling indestructible—as if I had taken something a lot stronger than a multi-vitamin. I had to hold back from skipping through the parking lot to the front door.

I was in love with everyone and everything. I had all the answers. I could predict everyday events in the office and at home. I gave my boss advice that I would not ordinarily have given. It was like a miracle, but a little scary.

My kids avoided me. My coworkers wondered what was going on. My boss began to make himself scarce. But I simply laughed at them all because I knew something extraordinary was happening in my life. I was being nudged by God.

The words "now go and put your talents to good use" stayed with me. I began to write. I wrote feverishly for six weeks—on paper tablecloths in restaurants, in restrooms on toilet paper, at home during my favorite TV shows, during the night sitting on the toilet seat,

---

16   See Appendix Contributor Biographies

in the car while driving, in the car while *not* driving. I was making my husband nuts!

I took that nudge a step further and mailed the articles I was writing to local newspapers for publication. All were published.

After six weeks, however, the sensations disappeared as quickly as they came. I understood. It was impossible to go on in a state of euphoria, removed from the real world. I was, in fact, exhausted from lack of sleep.

My mornings became ordinary again: my ordinary kitchen table, my ordinary cup of coffee, my ordinary robe. Even the Upper Room stories came across as ordinary.

But that experience can be recalled in a heartbeat. I need merely to sit quietly, close my eyes tightly, and recall those few special moments when the hand of God reached out one ordinary day and touched my soul in an extraordinary way.

Trick or Treat Surprise
(Linda Fitzpatrick[17])

Growing up, I went in and out of foster care because my mother was mentally ill and my father was unable to parent appropriately. When I was seven, while we were still together as a family, I went to a woman's home where she held a Vacation Bible School in her backyard. One of the few things I remember about those days was the picture frame I made out of popsicle sticks surrounding a beautiful picture of Jesus.

In the fall, I went to the same woman's house for Halloween where God spoke to me. This woman gave me a white, black, and red sucker and told me what the colors represented. Black was for the sin in my life, red was for the blood Jesus shed for my sins, and white was for my clean heart no longer full of sin after I accepted Jesus as my Savior.

Jesus washed my sins away. I believe salvation is just that simple. I'm so thankful that this woman took the time to tell a pitiful little girl the salvation truth. I can't wait to meet her again in Heaven. Though I don't remember her name, I am certain I will know her when I see her again.

> ***Trust in the LORD with all your heart and lean not on your own understanding; in all your ways submit to him, and he will make your paths straight.***
> ***-Proverbs 3:5-6***

---

[17] See Appendix Contributor Biographies

It has been fifty-one years since that Halloween night, and I am just as sure of my Redeemer as ever. I know without a shadow of doubt I am His bride. I am saved by His beautiful grace, and I know I will live eternally with Him.

I pray that you may know this for yourself.

Give Up or Listen?

The following story by Tamara is beautiful in its simplicity. Sometimes we forget that God is aware of all our needs. This writer was a teenager when she wrote this and sees, early in her Christian walk, that God does answer even the simplest prayer. This story encourages me in realizing how much God loves us, right down to a little piece of metal.

Paperclip
(Tamara Payne[18])

For a while now, I've been going through some problems with myself and with friends, and it's been hard for me to see the light at the end of the tunnel. Still I've been trying to trust in God and praise Him for what He's done already, instead of focusing on what I think needs to be done.

Anyway, I was having another one of those nights of being overwhelmed by my problems and praying that Jesus would give me some encouragement. I was doing what I usually do when I'm down—reading through my favorite book of the Bible, Philippians. After reading some, I started crying because I'm emotional like that. Once again, I found myself thinking I needed a paper clip (I like to mark different books of the Bible that way, and I still needed one for Philippians). Then I jokingly said aloud, "God, if you could help me find a paper clip somewhere in this room, that would be great." I chuckled to myself, put my Bible away, and was about to go to sleep when something prompted me to look through my encouragement folder where I keep sweet letters and cards that people give me. After I had read a few, I started to cry again. When I picked up another card, something fell out of an envelope. I continued to read the card until I saw something shiny out of the corner of my eye. It was a paper clip just lying there, looking up at me. With tears flowing down my cheeks, I laughed as I picked it up, whispering to myself, "God, You really do have a sense of humor. Thank you, thank you very much!"

---

18   See Appendix Contributor Biographies

There in my room that night, that little paper clip was a reminder to me that God *does* hear my prayers—even the ones that I say sarcastically, and He provides because He loves me. That paperclip was a sign, and now I'm sure that everything is going to be okay!
Thank you Jesus!

Dave Anderson and I have been friends for more than five years. Several states separate us, but through our involvement with the National Multiple Sclerosis Society, Dave, his wife, Marian, my husband, Bob, and I have had the treasure of friendship. He mentioned this story to me on the phone, and I was truly touched that he would share his act of faith with me. He and I both know how important it is for people with MS to take one of the disease modifying drugs in the form of injections either daily, a few times a week, or weekly. When he told me he was worried his physician would not prescribe it for him, we both held our breath and prayed for a different outcome. God answered the prayers we sent him.

The Chapel
(Dave Anderson[19])

I have had Multiple Sclerosis (MS) for many years and count on the medication I take for my MS to keep me well. For reasons that are still somewhat unclear to me, the medical resource I use for my prescription decided to stop providing this medication. It's very expensive, so I rely on them for the medication I need. After being refused a refill, I asked for an appointment with another doctor to appeal the decision. I prepared for this meeting with all the documentation I could gather, but I knew that all the information may not be enough. The medical facility had a chapel near the lobby which was my last stop before going upstairs to see the doctor. I've always had a strong belief in the power of prayer, and this was a time I really needed help. I felt I could change their minds, but I needed the calm confidence that prayer and meditation gave me.

My hurdles weren't crossed over yet as the doctor I met with agreed with the previous decision. Then she brought in her supervisor, and we had a long talk about what it would mean if I stopped taking the medication I counted on. I can't tell you how relieved I was when he agreed to renew the prescription. I left the doctor's office and went immediately back to the chapel to give thanks to God for helping me through this difficult time. It gives me great peace of mind to know

---

[19] See Appendix Contributor Biographies

Nudges 33

that we are not alone in our life struggles.[20]

Unexpected Conversations
(Liz Thompson[21])

I love talking with others in all kinds of places: at a bus stop, in a waiting room at the doctor's office, in public places, during events, and on walks with my dog. People tease me saying I go into "reporter mode" when talking with others because I ask questions, possibly things others would resist asking, but I am truly interested in the answers and not just being nosy. I love hearing other people's stories and talking with children who love to chat about nonsensical things. It's pure enjoyment for me.

One particular day, I was waiting for my bus in a waiting area between two large automatic doors that slid open frequently while people came and went from the medical building. I could have sat on the seat on my walker, but a young man moved his personal items so I could sit next to him on the bright red metal bench. I thanked him and took his offer.

He had his arm in a sling. Since it was a medical building where physical therapy took place, I made an assumption he was there for therapy. He was quiet, polite, and unassuming in nature and about twenty years old.

"What did you do to your arm?" I asked smiling.

Fully expecting a sports injury detail, I was surprised when he said, "Cancer. I had cancer in my shoulder."

His accent told me he was not a native to the United States.

"I'm so sorry," I replied. "Were they able to get all the cancer?"

"Yes, they were. I was glad I didn't lose my arm," he flashed a disarming smile.

"You thought you would lose it then? The sling is for support?"

"Yes, for support. I'm still healing, and no chemo is necessary."

He told me his name was Lucas, and I told him mine. He went on to tell me he was from Germany and came to the States six months ago for a children's ministry opportunity in Columbus, Ohio, called Agora Ministries.

"I had a choice to go Brazil or the U.S. Obviously I chose the U.S." Lucas said."Are you glad you chose the U.S. since you ended up with cancer and needed medical treatment?"

He was glad and explained that he had excellent care at the Ohio

---

20 See Appendix: Suggested Reading and Websites
21 See Appendix Contributor Biographies

State University Hospital. He had no regrets on his choice.

"I go home in a month, in time for Christmas," he said, looking down.

"It will be good to be home, won't it Lucas?"

"Yes, it will."

"I think God is watching over you and sent you here for a reason. Good that you were listening," I said with a smile.

He smiled, nodded, and said his ride had arrived.

"God bless you, Liz," were Lucas's last words to me.

God bless you, too, Lucas.

Later, I looked up Agora Ministries and found out that it is an inner-city ministry. I found out that Agora Christian Services, Inc. was organized as a Job Training Program for disadvantaged adults. Their mission statement discusses how their desire is to "empower young men and women, excluding no one, to develop their God given skills to become productive, self-supportive, and joyful people through the relationships with and the training by Christian men and women."[22]

WHISPERS

Whispers are when a child or grandchild cups his or her hands around their lips and moves in close to your ear. You feel it more than hear it. Even reading this and thinking about it, my guess is that you are smiling.

Are you remembering all the times as a child when you whispered to a friend, a parent, a grandparent, aunt or uncle? Maybe you remember the game "Telephone." In this game, friends sit in a circle and one person whispers something in the next person's ear. The message is repeated until the last person in the circle hears it. It is his or her job to tell everyone the message. Laughter usually rings out when a jumbled, nonsensical message was relayed such as "The elephant next to you is green?" instead of "The telephone is going to ring."

Whispering is so quiet that the message is often misunderstood. Yet there is a kind of intimacy in whispering like no other form of communication.

As children, we whispered to our friends or siblings, typically when we weren't supposed to be talking, such as in class or church, or when we didn't want anyone else to hear. Think back to the first day of school each year. You might have been wearing a new outfit

---

[22]   For more information see agoraministries.org

and probably new shoes and you were on your best behavior, hoping to start the school year off right with your new teacher.

It was 1959 or close to it, and the first day of third grade for me at Whittier Elementary School in Westerville, Ohio. A friend was leaning over toward me from her desk, talking to me about something. I knew we were not to be talking, and I whispered, apparently too loudly, "We're not supposed to talk!" Of course, my teacher heard me, and I was told to stand in the corner. The humiliation was too much when she said to the class, "Just ignore her."

Whispers are similar for adults but take on different meaning. Secrets seem to be told in whispers.

Does God whisper? The mightiest whispers come from God. The question is: are we listening?

In the following verses, the Bible shows us boldly how God might get our attention in ways we least expect as He talks to Elijah.

The LORD said, "Go out and stand on the mountain in the presence of the LORD, for the LORD is about to pass by." Then a great and powerful wind tore the mountains apart and shattered the rocks before the LORD, but the LORD was not in the wind. After the wind there was an earthquake, but the LORD was not in the earthquake. After the earthquake came a fire, but the Lord was not in the fire. And after the fire came a gentle whisper. When Elijah heard it, he pulled his cloak over his face and went out and stood at the mouth of the cave. Then a voice said to him, "What are you doing here, Elijah?"
-1 Kings 19:11-13

The King James Version says "still, small voice," in place of whisper, but the point is, God whispered to Elijah. Even as the earth exploded apart and fire surrounded him, God spoke softly into Elijah's ear, into his heart. Why did God do that? I think it is because Elijah did not expect a whisper. Like a child who sees the parent as the authority, we seldom expect a whisper when life all around is in turmoil.

God speaks to each of us differently. He wants our attention, and He wants to keep it forever. This world is a noisy place, filled with distractions that keep us from concentrating on eternal things. John Wesley's commentary suggests that the still voice is used "To intimate, that God would do his work in and for Israel in his own time, not by might or power, but by his own spirit." It goes on to describe the Holy Spirit moving "with a powerful, but yet with a sweet and gentle gale."[23]

Silence is difficult for many people. My personal silence came about gradually until I was deaf by fifty. It would be a year after my teacher put me in the corner for whispering too loudly that hearing loss was found in my young ears.

I had to learn to live in silence while the world was booming around me. Now, with two cochlear implants, I hear the noise, but I also adore the sounds and understand the words. It's a blessing I thank God for every day.

More times than I can count, God has reached me in this silence. He still whispers to me, and my prayer is that I will constantly listen.

There was a time, from 1987 to about 1993, when God woke me from sleep with words and melody for songs he gave me. Sleep would not return until I had taken my guitar in hand, plucked the song, and written the words and chords.

He also got my attention with the songs when I was in a place I could not stop and write. Driving a car, in the shower, on a walk, and other unlikely places, I might not have pen and paper handy. After this time in my life, more poems would come to me, and eventually I would write essays which led to column writing in 1998.

I would sing these songs in our little church we were part of in these days. There was a special woman I met when I was a church secretary at Linworth United Methodist Church in North Columbus, Ohio: Louise Thompson. She was a poet and storyteller. We shared a last name and a love for the Lord. We visited retirement centers and nursing homes where she would tell her stories and read her poems. I would sing my songs, and we would pray with the people. It was an inspiring time in my life, and I am grateful to have had that connection with Louise.

Louise's service to the Lord was long and full of love. Elmwood's Mite Society or Ladies Aid was organized in 1886. They met in homes until 1911 when a Ladies Aid Room was added to the church. Meeting twice a month on Thursday nights, the Society was a vital part in the growth of Linworth United Methodist Church. Longtime members were honored in 1957 with a Christmas Party at the home of Louise Thompson. "These wonderful women became known to many of us as Linworth's Lovely Ladies. Not only were they active in Ladies Aid, they were founding members of the Thimble Club in the early 1900's," Louise said in a

---

23   Cited information on John Wesley's Commentary; biblestudytools.com/commentaries/wesleys-explanatory-notes/1-kings/1-kings-19.html?p=2

newsletter for the church.

Rejoice
(Louise Thompson[24])

> I knew God was speaking,
> But I heard no loud voice,
> Just a sweet simple whisper
> That was saying, "Rejoice—
> Rejoice in your blessings
> That come every day,
> Make room for the miracles
> Coming your way.
> Look around and enjoy
> Wherein you've been placed
> And know you are there
> Just because of My Grace.
> Rejoice—with thanksgiving,
> In Christ take your stand,
> And you will be safe
> In the palm of My Hand."

Usually, when I sang my songs, people would comment about the songs and ask me questions on how I was inspired. Some people seemed in awe of my ability, but I always turned the attention to God. Again, it's not about me. God sent me on this journey for a reason, and He had a purpose. One Sunday, as I was practicing at home on our back porch, I knew God wanted me to sing a different song. I remember saying aloud, "But I just wrote that yesterday! I need more practice." The feeling that I needed to sing this song would not go away. God was persistent in this nudge. I sang the song He had given to me in church that day. Afterwards, a woman I had never seen before and never saw again came up to me and said, "How did you know I needed to hear that?" I was stunned, but then it all made sense to me. God knew she would be there and knew what she needed to hear. That was why He gave me the song the day before. As she stood there expectantly, I said, "I didn't know. God gave me that song yesterday."

"Yesterday?" she replied with her brow furrowed.

"Yes, and this morning I was planning on singing another song, but God told me to sing this one. Apparently for you," I added with a smile.

We were both in awe of God's plan. I still am.

---

24 See Appendix Contributor Biographies

Jelly and Kleenex

Grocery shopping can be a tedious task—sorting coupons, keeping children under control, busy schedules, and too little money. When my daughter was young, we did most of our shopping on the way home from my work and her day care center. As she got older, I taught her how to read coupons and look for the items in the store. She became a wise shopper and looked for the best prices. We would write the grocery list by mentally walking the aisles of our favorite store, Big Bear. It has since met its demise, but we spent hours shopping at these stores in whatever location was close to home or convenient on the way home.

As my daughter got older, I often went shopping alone. One time, I noticed the store had been rearranged and my aisle-by-aisle list was useless. There was a very short older woman reaching with all her might for something. I asked her if I could help, and her reply was, "Why do they change everything like this? Now I can't reach my jelly!" I hid a chuckle and reached, with effort since I'm only five foot four, her jelly. We chatted about how it makes shopping hard when the stores change things so drastically.

Another time, walking down the paper product aisle in the same store, I was looking at a coupon when I heard a sniffle. Then another. I looked toward the noise and saw a woman slightly younger than me standing in front of boxes of facial tissue (I always call them Kleenex) crying. Tears streamed down her face, and her shoulders moved in rhythm with her quiet sobs. Not quite sure what I ought to do, but knowing there was no way I was going to walk away from her, I remember asking God very quickly what to say. Now I realize that God had put me in that place, and even with my poor hearing, he allowed me to hear her crying and see her body language.

Moving closer to her, I said, "Are you OK? Can I help you?"

Her red, ringed eyes looked at me as she said, "I'm a terrible mother!"

"Why do you say that?"

"My stepchildren hate me. I can't do anything right."

The timing of her comment hit me like a rock, and I hid a smile. I had been struggling with my seventeen year old stepson because he was throwing clean, folded clothes down the laundry chute. I had just told him, after this had gone on for a time, that he would have to do all his own laundry from then on. Standing next to this distraught stepmother, I felt a kinship. I knew God placed me there for her and for me.

"I'm a stepmother, too. If you tell me what happened, maybe I will understand and can help you."

I truly don't remember her reply. It was more than twenty years ago. I do remember sharing a few stories, laughing a little, talking about how hard it was to be a stepparent when the children tested us all the time. All we want to do is love them and care for them. We parted with a smile, but not before we both grabbed a couple boxes of tissue and tossed them into our carts.

Having something in common helps with conversations the one just mentioned and helps form friendships. This next story was written by a women I met because we are both writers, Christians and happen to be living with MS. When I told her about my book and asked if she had anything to contribute, she didn't miss a beat and sent me the following.

Sorrow Leads to Writing Catharsis (And a book)
(Vicki Julian[25])

Does God work in my life? Oh, let me count the ways! So many times, I have felt God working through me to help others that it is difficult to single out any one particular event. But I know when it happens because there is no other feeling like it. Perhaps my most poignant experience was when God used me to help myself and to touch others in the long run.

I was facing the second Christmas without my beloved husband. The first Christmas occurred just three months after losing him, so I was still very much in shock. The second time, I knew what to expect, and it wasn't pleasant. As the holidays approached, I felt myself going in and out of excited anticipation countered with extreme sadness. One night, the overwhelming feeling of loss was so intense that I could not be comforted with the usual coping mechanisms of reading the Bible, listening to religious music, or watching inspirational movies. I finally concluded that relief could only come from going to my computer and writing a letter to my husband as I had done many times before.

But this time was different. As I sat down to write, a story emerged. I didn't write short stories. In my former business life, I wrote grants, explanatory manuals, guides, and business documents. However, after sitting and writing three hours straight, there it was! I had no idea where the story was going or how it would end when I began writing, but strangely enough, I found comfort in it. It was the story of an ethereal angel intervention. Over the course of the next four weeks, nine other stories were created in the same manner, all with interventions by either ethereal angels or humans given an angelic task to perform in answer to a prayer from someone in crisis. Truly, it felt as though these stories were written through me rather than by me. In fact, I'm certain of it. Each of the main characters in the stories felt extremely personal

---

25 See Appendix Contributor Biographies

to me. I could understand their thoughts, their wants, and their need for comfort even though we seemingly had nothing in common.

After encouragement from family and friends, the book was published under the most extraordinary circumstances, but that is another story for another time. What is most important, however, was hearing how the book had touched many readers and brought comfort to them. God had most assuredly given words of comfort through me, not only for me, but also for others.

I love it when others share theses experiences, and this book is blessed with poems and stories from others who have written about these moments. One such woman, Jan Widman, I met at Bible Study Fellowship. She often had long and interesting answers to our group questions. One time, as she read something she'd written, I chuckled and said, "Jan, send that to me for my book."

Whisper
(By Jan Widman[26])

>God whispers in a still small voice,
>And He doesn't do it every day.
>But when His words come to my ears,
>I'm attentive to hear what He will say.
>Sometimes His words are admonishing,
>Reminding me I'd best make a change.
>If I'm prudent, I'll tuck those away
>And follow the suggestions without shame.
>Then again that still small voice
>Offers whispers of comfort in my ears.
>Life's situations may have been oh so bleak;
>His voice gives me courage, not fear.
>I remember a night when I prayed as I drove.
>The night was snowy, treacherous and late.
>Reaching home safely, I gave Him hearty thanks.
>I heard "You're welcome," as I stepped from my car.
>Standing at the airport boarding gate, ready to fly,
>I was tearful and fearful thinking, "What had I done?"
>A myriad of dialect sounds enhancing my fear
>A touch and my name—no one was near—except Jesus the Son.
>Standing in the churchyard on a warm June day,
>I had just released my sins at the cross
>While walking out I heard His voice.

---

26   See Appendix Contributor Biographies

"You'll be a nurse," and I knew who would be my Boss.
God whispers in a still small voice,
And He doesn't do it every day.
But when His words come to my ears,
I must be attentive to hear what he will say.

Warning Whispers

Have you ever been in a situation and knew you had to escape? You knew the danger was real, even though you couldn't put your finger on it. Marsha, a friend of mine, told me this has happened many times in her life. Once she was driving on a freeway when her car sputtered, and she coasted it to the edge of the road. She called her husband and waited in the car. Shortly after pulling over, a man stopped and came up to the car under the premise of offering assistance.

Instantly, Marsha knew he could not be trusted. She felt the danger, edginess, and desire to flee. He offered to get in the car and try to start it, but she told him her husband should be there at any time.

She knew he meant to harm her. Even while telling the story, her hands shook.

What happened next had to be God's protection. A young man pulled over and asked if he could help, and the first man quickly got in his car and drove away. Marsha said she felt at ease with the second man, especially when the other one fled so quickly.

We do need to heed these "feelings," "premonitions," or whatever you might call it because often they are warnings in the form of a nudge to get us to safety.

Glad I Listened[27]
(Liz Thompson[28])

Most of my work life was good. From 1978 to 1987, I was fortunate to work at Battelle Memorial Institute in Columbus, Ohio. I began at entry level with my secretarial work and soon moved to more responsibility. The man who gave me a chance, even when others said he should not, was Michael Tikson. He managed the computer department and was a retired U.S. Air Force colonel.

He was quite tall with white, wavy hair and a ready smile. When I

---

27   Originally printed in Liz's first book, *Day by Day, the Chronicles of a Hard of Hearing Reporter,* 2008, published by Gallaudet University Press
28   See Appendix Contributor Biographies

interviewed to work for him, my competition was stiff. Many women had much more experience than I did. His secretary, Barbara Weed, was retiring and was hoping I would fill her spot.

One day, Mr. Tikson came to my office door and said, "Liz, will you come with me?" Of course I did. We walked down the long hallway on the 10th floor of Building 11, and he said he wanted to offer me the job of department secretary. He was talking, but my mouth was stuck open. I was amazed he had chosen me, a twenty-five year old, fairly naïve woman.

When we sat in his office, he smiled and said, "You do want the job, don't you?" Then, I realized I had not said a word and replied with an emphatic "Yes!"

He said other managers had advised him not to hire me, due to my inexperience, but I would learn that Mr. Tikson had his own mind. He apparently saw something in me others had not; he believed in me and said so.

I worked diligently for him from 1979 until we moved to Seattle in 1987. He received promotions and took me with him, making my last job title that of executive secretary. My hearing was waning slowly, but he and I never had any difficulty.

Shortly after I left, he retired from Battelle. Evan Brill, another manager whom I had worked with, contacted me in Seattle to let me know he was throwing a party for him and asked if I could make it. Over the course of his career, Mr. Tikson had only four secretaries, and Evan was trying to get us all there.

After being diagnosed with MS, I knew many people in Ohio were concerned about me, so Bob and I flew back for the party, surprising everyone but Evan. It was a great party, and after we visited family, we headed home to Seattle.

One year, shortly before Secretary's Day in April, Mr. Tikson called saying he wanted to take me out to lunch. I was doing database work then with very little secretarial work, and my poor hearing was a big issue at my current job. But he and I had a great lunch and caught up on how our grown children were doing.

When our daughter, Mary, was married in 1995, the Tiksons came and celebrated with us. He was sporting a gray beard and looking statelier than ever. This would be the last time I would see him until 1999.

The following column, published in *Suburban News Publications* and in my first book, is very special to me, and I hope I always remember the day when God gave me the ability to hear well enough to listen to a dying man's loving words.

I'M GETTING BETTER AT SAYING GOOD-BYE

Saying good-bye has always been difficult for me. Recently, I went to say good-bye to a dear friend of more than twenty years. He was a mentor, teacher, inspiration, but most of all a true friend, accepting of everyone. When I went to his home, I did not know what to expect about his illness. I had not asked prior to the visit, assuming his heart had weakened more—only physically, not spiritually. When I saw him bed ridden and looked into his eyes, I saw him there.

We held hands and talked, talked about what matters in this life, nothing trivial. We each had things to say to one another that could not be left unsaid. I don't think I blinked more than once. He was weak, and I concentrated on his every word, on every gentle squeeze he made with his hand, his inner turmoil in working to communicate so I could understand. It was not easy for either of us, but so necessary. For the next twenty-four hours, it was all I could think about; I dreamt about our visit and awoke with it on my mind. I didn't find that troublesome because it was a profound experience that I never want to forget.

My emotions are a mixture of loss, sadness, and extreme fulfillment. Loss of someone important for almost half of my life thus far, sadness that he was so ill, but fulfillment that I followed God's insistence that I overcome any of my personal fears and meet certain death in the face. My friend told me that he was not afraid to die, that he was ready. Even in his impending death, this giving man was still teaching me. He was showing me how to die without fear and how to leave this life on earth with grace and honor. I know God met him and said, "Well done, my good and faithful servant."

How unselfish he was with the little time we spent together. His words were meant to comfort me, and if I turned the conversation toward him, he would smile weakly, say "But . . .", and turn it back to me. We both needed this time to say good-bye.

The hospice was praised by the family. They were working with his young grandchildren to create a memory book of Papa. Counseling and medical explanations were readily available. This is not the first time I have heard such praise of similar hospices. My friend's wife and I talked about what special people the caretakers are. How giving, loving, dedicated, and selfless they are. I know sleep must be difficult for some of them to achieve, at times. When sleep and rest do engulf them, I like to think angels soothe them and allow slumber to renew their souls.

My dear friend has now moved on to a new life, one we can only dream about. He left a loving family, friends who loved him, and a wealth of memories and legacy for us to remember him by. His life enriched others because of his integrity, love of family and friends, encouragement, teaching, availability, laughter, and warm smile. He was successful in every definition of the word.
With his good-bye to me, my life's journey has taken yet another turn. I like to think of it as my soul's journey with God. I have learned to lose any fear of moving on and seeing what is around the next bend in my road. When I take my final glance at this life, I like to think he will be waiting. He will take my hand again, squeeze it gently, and say, "I am glad you listened."
So am I.

I encourage you to keep track of your life experiences and pass them on to loved ones. Journaling, scrapbooking, blogging online, photography, and letter writing are a few suggestions.

3

Fudges

If I didn't have spiritual faith, I would be a pessimist. But I'm an optimist. I've read the last page in the Bible. It's all going to turn out all right.
-Billy Graham[29]

No one is perfect. If we think back to our past, most likely our lives have been riddled with missed opportunities or times when we wished for a "do over," another chance, or a way to somehow make it right. Movies abound with this theme of someone wishing he or she could go back and do things differently. In the real world, it's not possible to go back, but our experiences can teach us to stop us from repeating these missed moments. Just as the rough, steep hills give strength to our leg muscles, the same goes for the heart, mind, and soul. Over many decades, I've had many types of fudges that have opened my eyes to missed opportunities. Learning the hard way has been a theme throughout my life.

I think Satan dances when we decide we know better than God does. Because he thrives on our fudges, I believe we need to understand him better to be able to keep him out of our lives. Many of our missed opportunities might have occurred because he had too much of a sway in our private thoughts. That is why we need to understand our adversary and discover how we can keep him at bay.

THE WHOLE ARMOR OF GOD

Finally, be strong in the Lord and in his mighty power. Put on

---

29 See Appendix: Quote References

the full armor of God, so that you can take your stand against the devil's schemes. For our struggle is not against flesh and blood, but against the rulers, against the authorities, against the powers of this dark world and against the spiritual forces of evil in the heavenly realms. Therefore put on the full armor of God, so that when the day of evil comes, you may be able to stand your ground, and after you have done everything, stand. Stand firm then, with the belt of truth buckled around your waist, with the breastplate of righteousness in place, and with your feet fitted with the readiness that comes from the gospel of peace. In addition to all this, take up the shield of faith, with which you can extinguish all the flaming arrows of the evil one. Take the helmet of salvation and the sword of the Spirit, which is the word of God. And pray in the Spirit on all occasions with all kinds of prayers and requests. With this in mind, be alert and always keep on praying for all the Lord's people. Pray also for me, that whenever I speak, words may be given so that I will fearlessly make known the mystery of the gospel, for which I am an ambassador in chains. Pray that I may declare it fearlessly, as I should.
-Ephesians 6:10-20

    When my first grandson, Jacob, was very young, his parents got him an Armor of God play set from a Christian store. He had a thick plastic breastplate, a helmet, and a sword. It was humorous to see him parading around in it, but his parents, Bob and Mary, made sure he understood the implications of the garments. Now he is a strong Christian who displays a love for others that is comforting to this grandmother's heart. He and his siblings were taught early on to love God first.

    We need to put on this armor every day to prevent Satan from getting close to us. The Scripture creates a clear picture, ".with the belt of truth buckled around your waist, with the breastplate of righteousness (being honorable and honest; adhering to moral principles) in place, and with your feet fitted with readiness that comes from the gospel of peace... take up the shield of faith... the helmet of salvation and the sword of the Spirit..." In addition, we are to pray at all times. Not some of the time or when it's convenient, but at all times.

EVEN SATAN BELIEVES

Satan, the Hinderer, may build a barrier about us, but he can

never roof us in, so that we cannot look up.
-J. Hudson Taylor[30]

You most likely have seen the banners, garden rocks, wall hangings, and the like that state, "Believe." At first, my thought was that Christian beliefs were making inroads into secular marketing. However, in time, I realized it was a catch phrase and could be used to remind you to believe any old thing.

Remember, even Satan believes in God and Jesus, but he wants to replace them, not honor them. He is the father of all lies and a murderer: "You belong to your father, the devil, and you want to carry out your father's desire. He was a murderer from the beginning, not holding to the truth, for there is no truth in him. When he lies, he speaks his native language, for he is a liar and the father of lies" (John 8:44). He is also our adversary (enemy): "Be alert and of sober mind. Your enemy the devil prowls around like a roaring lion looking for someone to devour" (1 Peter 5:8). He lied to Eve in the Garden of Eden, and because she listened, life as it should have been, changed.

Satan tempted Jesus, unsuccessfully, and he tempts us today. If he didn't believe, there would be no need for him to be our enemy. He was one of God's angels and formed an army to take over in Heaven. God threw him out, and now he lurks on this earth. But the good news is that, in the book of Revelations, we are told that Satan will be thrown into the bottomless pit when Jesus comes again.

Billy Graham's book, "Angels,"[31] is a valuable read for confirming beliefs of who Satan is. If we understand better whom we are fighting, we will be better prepared with a defense.

Satan has many names.[32] Graham writes, "The apostle Paul understood and spoke of the war of rebellion in the heavens when he referred to the former Lucifer, now Satan, as 'the prince of the power of the air, the spirit that now worketh in the children of disobedience' (Ephesians 2:2)."[33] We need to be aware of his ways so we can be ready to push him aside.

In chapter six of Graham's book, "Lucifer and the Angelic Rebellion," he spells out what happened in Heaven when Lucifer decided he wanted to be God. Graham writes, "Many people ask, 'How could this conflict come about in God's perfect universe?' The apostle Paul calls it 'the mystery of iniquity.' 2 Thessalonians 2:7 'For the mystery

---

30   See Appendix: Quote References
31   Billy Graham, Angels, U.S., Word Publishing, 1994
28   http://www.abecedarian.org/Pages/namesofsatan.htm
29   Ibid, Pages 67-68

of lawlessness is already at work. Only he who now restrains it will do so until he is out of the way.'

While we have not been given as much information as we might like, we do know one thing for certain: The angels who fell, fell because they had sinned against God. In 2 Peter 2:4 the Scripture says, 'God spared not the angels that sinned but cast them down to hell, and delivered them into chains of darkness, to be reserved unto judgment.'

'Thus, the greatest catastrophe in the history of the universal creation was Lucifer's defiance of God and the consequent fall of perhaps one-third of the angels who joined him in his wickedness."[34]

In Isaiah 14:12-14, the origin of the conflict is recorded,

"How you have fallen from heaven, morning star, son of the dawn! You have been cast down to the earth, you who once laid low the nations! You said in your heart, 'I will ascend to the heavens; I will raise my throne above the stars of God; I will sit enthroned on the mount of assembly, on the utmost heights of Mount Zaphon, I will ascend above the tops of the clouds; I will make myself like the Most High.'"

Satan was, and is, filled with himself as displayed with the repeated "I"s in these verses.

No matter how this world wants to downplay Satan's role, he is on this earth, and he is working to pull the rug from underneath anyone willing to listen to his deceit. He delights when we fall, stumble, and doubt God's Word. John 8:44 tells us he is the father of lies. Each of us must realize that Satan is real even though we cannot see him; he is evident in all of the sin on this earth. Graham writes, "Sin is the frightful fact in our world. It writes its ruin in vice and lust, in the convulsions of war, in selfishness and sorrow, and in broken hearts and lost souls. It remains as the tragedy of the universe and the tool of Satan to blunt or destroy the works of God."[35]

Thinking and talking about Satan can be oppressive and discouraging, but there is hope! When we turn from our sin and walk into Jesus' arms, He will protect us from Satan and give us new life. We must turn to Christ in faith and trust, confess our sins—that's right, tell God even though He already knows—and ask Him to forgive you. Satan wants us to trust ourselves, not God, and he works daily to hiss in our ear with false promises. Graham writes, "Listen to Satan's 'ifs' of death being injected into the minds of people today: 'if' you live a good life, 'if' you do what is right, 'if' you go to church, 'if' you work for the benefit of others--if, if, if. However, the Bible teaches that these 'ifs' are not enough to meet God's requirements for salvation. Our

---

34 Ibid, Pages 67-68
35 Ibid, Page 75

good works and intentions are not enough. Jesus said, 'You must be born again'" (John 3:7).[36]

Putting aside all these words which may seem like a foreign language to you, know this: God made you, He has a purpose for you, and if we trust Him and listen, He will show you the way. We need to listen to God's whispers and ignore Satan's hisses and temptations. God will not tempt us because He wants what is best for us. Satan only wants to draw us away from God because he wants to *be* God. He wants his army of evil to grow in numbers to overthrow God and His angels in heaven. We must choose.

He Shows me the Way
(Liz Thompson)

> He shows me the way
> Each and every day.
> He shows me the way
> Every time I pray.
> Walking toward the light,
> What a blessed sight!
> Jesus is the light;
> Keep walking toward the light.
> **Chorus:**
> He will be right there,
> Holding out His arms.
> Showing that He cares.
> With a love that's warm.
>
> He'll show you the way
> Each and every day.
> He'll show you the way
> Every time you pray.
> The Spirit is your guide
> Always there inside.
> Jesus' walking there;
> Tell Him your fears and cares.
> **Chorus:**
> He will be right there.
> Holding out His arms,
> Showing that He cares,
> With a love that's warm.

---

[36] Ibid, Page 77

Keep walking toward the light, friends. This light will shine, and Satan will run because he is the father of dark.

Satan watches for those vessels that sail without convoy.
-George Swinnock[37]

The trouble with nearly everybody who prays is that he says "Amen" and runs away before God has a chance to reply. Listening to God is far more important than giving Him your ideas.
-Frank Laubach[38]

Fudges

For you were once darkness, but now you are light in the Lord. Live as children of light (for the fruit of the light consists in all goodness, righteousness and truth) and find out what pleases the Lord. Have nothing to do with the fruitless deeds of darkness, but rather expose them... But everything exposed by the light becomes visible—and everything that is illuminated becomes a light. This is why it is said: 'Wake up, sleeper, rise from the dead, and Christ will shine on you.' Be very careful, then, how you live—not as unwise but as wise, making the most of every opportunity, because the days are evil.
-Ephesians 5:8-16

This verse ends saying "making the most of every opportunity." This is a concept that every believer wants to learn. One of the first times I remember not doing something when I felt sure God wanted me to act was in the early 1980's. My daughter and I were shopping at J.C. Penney's at a shopping center in Columbus, Ohio. Being a smaller store, I could easily wander through and find a nice gift, have my daughter's picture taken, buy some essentials, or just look.

That day, I was buying a gift for someone. Now more than once, I have embarrassed family by chatting with strangers in almost any situation. Standing at the checkout, waiting behind another person, I noticed the clerk seemed tired, frustrated, or distracted.

I felt sure that I was to encourage this clerk somehow which was usually easy for me to do but not that day. I balked. After making my purchase and walking to the car with my daughter, I felt a pull to go

---

37   See Appendix: Quote References
38   See Appendix: Quote References

back into the store and talk with her. Immediately, I realized we were late getting to wherever we were going. I still remember sitting in the driver's seat, dejected. I knew I had failed at something. Right then, I knew I had missed a chance to do something good.

God has placed me in diverse situations since then. He has given me many chances to follow-through on His plans. There have surely been times I didn't listen, misunderstood, or didn't have the confidence that God would use me. What we all must realize is that God will not place us in a situation we cannot handle; He will be there with us. When our human desire takes precedence over God's will, we most likely flub it and make a mess of the task. When we are doing something just to look good to others, everyone loses. In 1 Corinthians 10:13, the Bible tells us, when we are tempted, there is comfort, saying, "No temptation has overtaken you except what is common to mankind. And God is faithful; he will not let you be tempted beyond what you can bear. But when you are tempted, he will also provide a way out so that you can endure it." This verse speaks directly to our temptation to sin, but I think it also relates to being tempted to ignore doing what God wants us to do since it typically is caused by sin of selfishness or lack of confidence.

It's not about us.

Regrets are Teachers
(Kathleen Grimm Welty[39])

The tiny two-room apartment was her world. The few mementos from her previous seventy years hung, framed and organized, on one wall. Figurines of yesteryear stood on two coffee tables. She didn't drive, and she couldn't walk far, either. Edith Stanley was not focused on worldly goods and activities; she was drawn to her heavenward spiritual walk.

She had given me a most hospitable welcome to her home. Her rooms had been carved from the giant house she used to live in. She was a two-minute drive from our parsonage, and it was my pleasure to visit her. I admired her sweet way of decorating her small space interestingly and neatly. She was a clever lady.

She passed from this life to heaven, and I still have not been able to shake my regret. I had broken a promise to Edith.

I was in charge of the Mother/Daughter luncheon at church her last year. Long before the event, I made arrangements to give her a ride. But I forgot to pick her up.

---

39 See Appendix: Contributor Biographies

I know she must have dressed in her Sunday best and anticipated the warm fellowship that awaited her. She loved her two rooms, but her joy blossomed when surrounded by her church family.

But I didn't come.

How long did she sit in that small chair and watch out the window? At what point in time did I change from her beloved friend to a pastor's wife with no sense of responsibility? To some, it may not seem like a big deal, but to me, it was an enormous mistake. My heart ached that day when I realized I had failed Edith.

She never said those words. She didn't blame me or speak ill of me, but I have imagined that it would be impossible for her to feel otherwise. I was the one who had convinced her it was important for her to participate. After all, I had planned a great program and had made beautiful decorations. In addition, the food would be excellent, I had said to her. I had built it up. I had set her hopes for a wonderful Saturday.

My apology sounded lame. Its echo replayed in my memory and whittled into my heart, but it changed me.

Not long afterward, I read in the book *The Way They Learn*, by Cynthia Tobias, that there are categories of learning styles. It piqued my interest, and the more I read, the more I realized, I am not an auditory learner. My spoken promise to Edith, did not "stick" in my brain as a visual cue would have. If I say, "I will pick you up," but don't write myself a note, I am less likely to remember. It encouraged me that a correctable physical difficulty might cure some of my forgetfulness.

Then, at a ladies retreat, a workshop title reached out and grabbed me: Organize with a Daily Planner. I learned to write notes on my purse-size calendar and trained myself to check it daily.

Some family members think I am still forgetful, but without my visual cues, I would be worse! Since my path intersected with Edith's, I know in my heart that the whole situation was used for my good. I remember Edith's kindness and patience, and I remember calendar events, too.

A Missed Opportunity
(Vickie Julian[40])

I can still see her. Sitting on the floor of the post office next to the drop slot, she was taking refuge from the extreme cold. It was obvious that she was homeless, and with only a few strewn possessions around her, I felt compelled to help. I wanted to give her

---

40   See Appendix: Contributor Biographies

money, but I didn't know what I could do without offending her. So what did I do? Nothing! That lost opportunity to help a fellow woman has haunted me to this day.

Soon after this encounter, I realized that I could have dropped a wadded bill on the floor, picked it up, and then offered it to her as maybe something that was hers. Of course, I wouldn't be lying because it really would be hers after I gave it to her! But this thoughtful scenario came to me far after the opportunity had passed.

I looked for her every time that I had mail to drop off late in the evening, but she was never there again. I said a prayer asking God to watch over her and send someone to help her who would know how to respond in the moment. I vowed to never again waste an opportunity to help someone when I could. Since then, God has presented me with a number of situations where I could, and did, help someone in need. But most importantly, He keeps the memory of my failure to do what He was asking of me fresh in my mind. That "fudge" is now my constant "nudge" to obey when God calls.

Simple Acts Left Undone
(Sonja Stauch[41])

Peg and Pat were close friends of me and my husband when they lived in Ohio. Shortly after they moved to Georgia, my husband was diagnosed with Alzheimer's Disease. Peg visited me after I had to move Dick to a nursing home and was very concerned about how I was going to survive. She knew I was working full time, caring for Dick, and raising a teenage daughter. Peg's visit showed me that I had more support and strength that I thought possible.

As time passed after Peg's visit and her show of concern, I fell into a routine, finding myself coping better than I thought I could. Knowing friends like Peg and Pat were holding me up in prayer sustained me. Day grew into day, but I never called Peg to let her know how much her support kept me going and to tell her I was getting by with all the stress. "I'll wait until I have more than one thing to share with her," I would think to myself. "Peg knows I'm OK, and I'll let her know soon."

Soon did not come quickly enough because the next news I had about Peg and Pat was that a drunk driver had killed them. They died instantly. In that same instant, my opportunity to let

---

41   See Appendix: Contributor Biographies

Peg know how I was doing and how much she meant to me had passed. I carry the regret with me even today.

Another person who I missed an opportunity with was Annette, the honorary grandmother of my daughter, also Annette. She had been a widow for a month. Annette and her husband were married for more than fifty years. She was visiting her daughter, a good friend of mine, in Michigan. Again, I kept thinking I should call Annette to see how she was and tell her I planned to take her shopping whenever she needed. I also wanted to check on my friend.

Before I followed through on my good intentions, I received a call that Annette had died in her sleep. My pain and regrets were very difficult to bear. However, I do not want to live on regrets.

Today if I get an overwhelming thought of someone, I contact him or her. I don't wait for a convenient time or for the news to be significant. Everyone enjoys a call from a friend! I am learning to listen for that little voice because God works in small ways. I need to listen more when God tells me to do something even if it is something as simple as making a phone call or sending a card.

Our Adversary majors in three things: noise, hurry and crowds. If he can keep us engaged in 'muchness' and 'manyness,' he will rest satisfied.
-Richard J. Foster[42]

It is true that Satan wants to keep us so busy we don't have time to think about what is important. Julie's story below is a case of being too busy and making her day full of mini-disasters. This certainly is not what God wants for our days. Julie said that her biggest problem when it comes to "fudging" is that she always promises more than she can possibly deliver, trying to make everybody happy. Most of us can relate, even if our story is different.

Zigzag All Day Long
(Julie Lindsey[43])

That Saturday was a beautiful but awful day. I was taking care of my two young granddaughters, Lindsey and Lauren, and had offered to serve food to the volunteers at the annual school flower show. I put hot dogs in the slow cooker to take to the volunteers later that day. All day long, I alternated between dishing

---

42   See Appendix: Quote References
43   See Appendix: Contributor Biographies

Fudges

out food, grocery shopping, and getting my two charges to where they needed to go.

After I dropped them off at art class at nine in the morning, I went home to get Sam, our two-year old chocolate lab. He loves car rides. Once he was in the car, we headed out to pick up the girls at 9:45.

Sam escaped when I picked them up and zigzagged through the busiest street in town, coming close to the four-lane Main Street many times and running through several yards. I almost had heart failure. Because chasing him only made him run faster, Lindsey ran away from him, and he chased her. She somehow managed to step on his leash, and we stuffed him in the car. He was not remorseful.

We opted to take Sam home and picked up the hot dogs and cake for the teachers. We were taking the food into the school to serve, when I realized we were low on condiments and rushed back to the grocery. After I was back at the school, I realized I had left my jacket in the grocery cart and had to go to the store to get it.

After that, I had to go to Bay's Market, a few houses from the school, to get a small "mammoth" meat tray. I had ordered a small meat tray for the teachers, but the "small" was two feet wide and wouldn't even fit in the refrigerator! With all the food in place, finally, we served volunteers starting at 10:50.

Catching my breath, we left school at two, so my granddaughters' father could pick them up for ball practice after they gathered their things. That done, I went back to school to clean up. At 4:30, my friend, Susie, surprised us with a visit and ended up spending the night.

I was exhausted. What hot dogs were left in the slow cooker would also "die" there, getting cold sitting on the stovetop. While I was at church the next day, Sam pulled the pot off the stove, shattering it into a million pieces, and ate the hot dogs. Besides the mess to clean up, sleep was a problem that night because I was afraid that Sam had swallowed some of the crockery and would bleed internally. I stayed up most of that night watching him to make sure he was OK. He never did seem to suffer any ill effects, thank the Lord! I was so tired that I cried, but I did make it to work the next day.

I realized that this was a small slice of how my daughter, Molly, lives her whole life. I gained a new admiration for the energy she uses for her family. Since that day, I have made sure that I never again had so much to deal with at one time. I certainly learned from this fudge of a day. Each event and person in my day only got a small slice of my time and attention.

Looking back on this one day, I can see this is not the way God intended for life to be. He wants us to "be still" and seek Him, not wearing ourselves out on things of little importance.

Quiet Destruction
(Liz Thompson)

Our pastor told a story about a young man who asked a seasoned farmer why his barn was falling down. "Why didn't you fix it before this happened?"

The farmer answered, "Well, when it was sunny and dry, it didn't seem to need repair, but when it rained, it leaked and fell apart. But I couldn't work on it then because of the weather."

As our bodies age, it's obvious we are under quiet physical destruction like the farmer's barn. Most of us live as healthfully as we can, taking our vitamins, getting some exercise, and keeping the bad habits at bay as much as possible, but no one is perfect, even if we consider ourselves health enthusiasts.

Accidents, injuries, and illness happen regardless of precautions we take. As an ER nurse said to me when I explained how I broke my wrist, "Well, that's why they call it an accident!" My body has been under quiet destruction for years as multiple sclerosis worked its silent damage. I take the injections proven to slow progression, err on the side of caution to prevent accidents, and take care of my body, mind, and spirit, but that's about all I can do.

An interesting thing has happened as the MS has slowed me down—I have more time for reflection, prayer, and soul-enriching reading. My discernment has grown stronger as I take the time to think things through. The fact that I was deaf by fifty also slowed me down enough to learn how to listen to the world around me. I now have two successful cochlear implants and have a renewed love of sounds—in particular, the clarity of speech and sounds of nature.

Silence and time for reflection have changed (for the better) how I see my life and the lives of others around me. I have a new ability to look inside my heart and toss out extraneous baggage weighing me down, repairing broken places.

I can see the loose nails and rotting boards in my life sooner, and I've learned to ask God to help me clean up my act. Sometimes old sins come back to haunt me, but only until I realize those have already been forgiven and Satan is just trying to use every hidden thought to break me down. If I put garbage into my brain, then that is what will come out when I act or react.

I choose to read books and watch movies by those who realize a story can be told in such a way that anyone could read or watch it without embarrassment. Seldom are these movies on the bestselling list.

The challenge is real today to keep a pure heart and mind when we are bombarded daily with what I call "R-rated actions." If you don't experience it personally, turn on your TV or computer and watch the news.

Another story explains clearly how easy it is to put off cleaning up our own lives when we see the filth in others' lives.

A young couple moved into a new neighborhood. The next morning while they were eating breakfast, the young woman saw her neighbor hanging the wash outside. "That laundry is not very clean," she said. "She doesn't know how to wash correctly. Perhaps she needs better laundry soap."

Her husband looked on but remained silent.

Every time her neighbor would hang her wash to dry, the young woman would make the same comments.

About one month later, the woman was surprised to see a nice clean wash on the line and said to her husband, "Look, she has learned how to wash correctly. I wonder who taught her."

The husband said, "I got up early this morning and cleaned our windows."

And so it is with life. What we see when watching others depends on the purity of the window through which we look.

In the first story, the young man saw clearly that the farmer could have prevented his barn's collapse. In addition, the young woman made incorrect assumptions about another when the solution was in a bottle of window cleaner and a rag of her own.

When we are tempted to complain or find fault in another, it might be wise to make sure we have a clean motive and have built a strong foundation, so we won't collapse in the process and take others down with us.

No temptation has overtaken you except what is common to mankind. And God is faithful; he will not let you be tempted beyond what you can bear. But when you are tempted, he will also provide a way out so that you can endure it.
-1 Corinthians 10:13

Surely, you realize that, in order for me to have this gem of knowledge, I had to experience the fallout of complaining. When asked, "How are you doing?" some people reply, "I can't complain."

My retort, at times, is, "Well, you can complain, but will it do any good?"

Complaining seems to be inborn in us, and it is up to us to shut our mouths and stop. It is our choice to find the good in any situation. Believe me when I say I know it's tough to do; I have struggled much of my life with either knowing I was whining or with the thoughts of whining. A baby, or young child, whines, "I want my Mommy!" or "I don't wanna!" As we mature, we may think these same thoughts but have learned it proves problematic; it doesn't solve a thing.

It is in the ordinary duties and labors of life that the Christian can and should develop his spiritual union with God.
-Thomas Merton[44]

---

44   See Appendix: Quote References

4

This Little Light of Mine

'Twas an unhappy Division that has been made between Faith and Works; though in my Intellect I may divide them, just as in the Candle I know there is both Light and Heat. But yet, put out the Candle, and they are both gone.
-John Selden[45]

Remember, a small light will do a great deal when it is in a very dark place. Put one little tallow candle in the middle of a large hall, and it will give a good deal of light.
-Dwight L. Moody[46]

When I read these quotes by Selden and Moody, I instantly think of this children's song "This Little Light of Mine." What a perfect song to teach our children. Did you learn it as a child possibly in Sunday school or Vacation Bible School? Since Jesus is the Light of the World, once we devote our lives to Him, His light shines through us. God's light, or His love, can shine through everything we do or say; it affects how we react to circumstances and how we act day to day.

Maybe this is a new concept for you, so bear with me. Scripture talks about this in the book of John.

> *If you love me, keep my commands. And I will ask the Father, and he will give you another advocate to help you and be with you forever—the Spirit of truth. The world cannot accept*

---
45 See Appendix: Quote References
46 See Appendix: Quote References

him, because it neither sees him nor knows him. But you know him, for he lives with you and will be in you. I will not leave you as orphans; I will come to you. Before long, the world will not see me anymore, but you will see me. Because I live, you also will live. On that day you will realize that I am in my Father, and you are in me, and I am in you. Whoever has my commands and keeps them is the one who loves me. The one who loves me will be loved by my Father, and I too will love them and show myself to them.
John 14:15-21

In these verses, Jesus tells us how we will receive a new comforter who is the Holy Spirit and He will live *in* us. I understand that to mean God is pouring His Spirit into us. This light being in us makes us shine, so we should let our light shine! We show the joy of knowing God is in us, guiding us, and shining through us by showing "…love, joy, peace, forbearance, kindness, goodness, faithfulness, gentleness and self-control" (Galatians 5:22-23) which are the fruits of the Spirit. God will not leave us as orphans because, once we have accepted Jesus into our hearts, we are adopted into the family of God with God as our Father. This reminds me of the Bill Gaither song, The Family of God.

The Family of God[47]
(Words and Music by William J. Gaither)

> I'm so glad I'm a part of the Family of God,
> I've been washed in the fountain, cleansed by His Blood!
> Joint heirs with Jesus as we travel this sod,
> For I'm part of the family,
> The Family of God
> You will notice we say "brother and sister" 'round here,
> It's because we're a family and these are so near;
> When one has a heartache, we all share the tears,
> And rejoice in each victory in this family so dear.

> **Chorus:**
> I'm so glad I'm a part of the Family of God,
> I've been washed in the fountain, cleansed by His Blood!
> Joint heirs with Jesus as we travel this sod,
> For I'm part of the family,
> The Family of God

---

47   See Appendix: Music Notes

From the door of an orphanage to the house of the King,
No longer an outcast, a new song I sing;
From rags unto riches, from the weak to the strong,
I'm not worthy to be here, but PRAISE GOD! I belong!

Chorus:
I'm so glad I'm a part of the Family of God,
I've been washed in the fountain, cleansed by His Blood!
Joint heirs with Jesus as we travel this sod,
For I'm part of the family,
The Family of God

Years ago, I was inspired to write a song about the fruits of the Spirit. I was struggling and wondering if anything I was doing was making a difference. When I read Galatians chapter five, the following song was given to me to comfort me and those who heard me sing it. I hope the words give you a measure of comfort as you read, knowing we plant the seeds for Christ and pray for a harvest whether we will see it or not.

Walk in the Spirit
(Liz Thompson)

If we live in the Spirit, let us walk in the light.
Let the fruits of the Spirit be our shining light,
For the world will only know us by the things that they see.
If we walk in the Spirit, maybe they'll join you and me.
The narrow path will lead you to the Son of righteousness
When the fruits of the Spirit are your daily bread.
Drink in all the lovely things that God provides for you,
And the fruits of the Spirit will flow out from you.
Oh, the fruits of the Spirit are a gift from our God;
We must be willing to receive the blessing of the heart.
Just close your eyes and say to Him "Let me be your own,"
And our loving God will hear you, and you'll never be alone.

Chorus:
Love and joy, let it shine. The world will not receive us, but we still must let it shine.
Love and joy—truth and peace. There's darkness all around us, but we still must let it   shine.
Love and joy—grace and peace.
What a wonderful Savior, what a beautiful Spirit, what a most

loving Lord, oh, let it shine.
Let us walk in the Spirit and walk as the children of the light.

Light and sunshine have been topics for hymn writers for years. Some that immediately come to mind are "Send the Light," "Sunshine in My Soul," "Unclouded Day," and Amy Grant's "Thy Word," based on Psalm 119:105, "Your word is a lamp for my feet, a light on my path." A quick concordance search shows that there are more than four hundred biblical references to light.

Another verse that clearly demonstrates this light and the fact it is not about us but Christ's love is 2 Corinthians 4:5-6, "For what we preach is not ourselves, but Jesus Christ as Lord, and ourselves as your servants for Jesus' sake. For God, who said, 'Let light shine out of darkness,' made his light shine in our hearts to give us the light of the knowledge of God's glory displayed in the face of Christ." One light in a dark room may illuminate the whole space. One candle shows the way in darkness. That is what God wants us to do with the love He has poured into our hearts. We need to let that love shine into the dark world and give others hope where they have none.

As children, we may think we are going to live forever, and time seems to move slowly. When we grow older, we read this Scripture and realize that God was working in us even as a child—especially as a child.

When I was young, I firmly believed that God and Jesus were one little man who lived in my heart. I never seemed to separate them in my mind; God and Jesus were one person. It felt like my secret, and I smile remembering how I felt. I learned that God knew my heart and that Jesus would come into my heart, if I invited Him.

Since Jesus Came into my Heart[48]

Since Jesus came into my heart,
Since Jesus came into my heart,
Floods of joy o'er my soul
Like the sea billows roll,
Since Jesus came into my heart.

As a girl, I did not really understand the true meaning of Jesus coming into my heart, but I interpreted it that He was actually there. I knew Jesus was always with me, and this way I was liter-

---

48   See Appendix: Music Notes

ally carrying Him in my heart. Whenever I saw pictures in Sunday school showing Jesus with children at His side. I wanted to be one of those children in the pictures.

CHILDLIKE FAITH

When I was a child, I talked like a child, I thought like a child, I reasoned like a child. When I became a man, I put the ways of childhood behind me. For now we see only a reflection as in a mirror; then we shall see face to face. Now I know in part; then I shall know fully, even as I am fully known.
-1 Corinthians 13:11-12

He called a little child to him, and placed the child among them. And he said: 'Truly I tell you, unless you change and become like little children, you will never enter the kingdom of heaven. Therefore, whoever takes the lowly position of this child is the greatest in the kingdom of heaven. And whoever welcomes one such child in my name welcomes me. If anyone causes one of these little ones—those who believe in me—to stumble, it would be better for them to have a large millstone hung around their neck and to be drowned in the depths of the sea."
-Matthew 18:2-6

Keeping these verses in mind, read on for letters children wrote to Jesus. I asked them to write what they would ask Jesus if they had a chance to sit with Him. These are unedited and purely the words and thoughts of these children.

Dear Jesus,

I love how you died on the cross to take our sins. I wish I never sin again. I know I've been sinning a lot but I do not want to sin ever again in my live.
Love,
Esther, 7

Dear Jesus,

If I could have just one wish, it would be to have one hour, just one hour, with you. A lot of verses in the Bible don't seem to make sense, but to be able to talk

with you and ask questions would take all my worries and doubts away. I have to admit, that sometimes when we sing the song "More Love to Thee" at church, I don't always sing the written words. When we come to the verse that goes, "This is my earnest plea: more love oh, Christ, to thee," I sing "This is my earnest plea; one hour alone with thee." My next wish is that everybody was a Christian and got along together. Wouldn't that make the world a lot better? Thank you for loving me, Jesus. Even though I might not get my wish until I'm in Heaven.
Love,
Beth, 11

Dear Jesus,

What is it like living in Heaven? I'm sure it's awesome. Thank you for dying for my sins. What was that like? How did it feel helping all those people like the blind and sick? I think it's amazing what you did for everyone. Thank you for answering my prayers and giving me strength when I ask for it. Is Heaven as beautiful as they say it is? Is it hard to answer everyone's prayers? Thank you so much for coming into my life and helping with my problems.
Love,
Megan

Dear Jesus,

I heard about you being crucified and you rised 3 days later. Today about 2010 years life is good. About one year ago I heard some scientists said that it was the beginning of the end, and about 3 months ago I heard that from between creation and Noahs ark their was about 2000 years. From Noah's ark till your birth was about 2000 years ago. From your birth to now it is about 2000 years. is it true Lord that you are coming back to save us? If it is close will it be before I die?
Love,
Andrew, 10
P.S. I'll see you soon!

Dear Jesus,

Will we recaniss ouir parins, friends and reliteves when we go to heven, because I know you want us to be happy there? Jesus you are allmitghy and powerful. Jesus will are pets and animals be in heven because I know you created them? Thank you for dieing on the cross for us.
Love,
Tyler, 10

Dear Jesus,

Thank you for dieing on the cross for our sins. Thank you for doing stuff for us. Your the best. You do stuff for us all and we are thankfull of that. I hope I see you one day in heaven.
Love,
Riley, 10

Dear Jesus,

Is baptisum the only way to get to heaven? Thank you for blessing me. Thank you for blessing me so I'm not pore.
Love,
Carter, 8

Dear Jesus,

This is Samantha, but you already knew that. I just want to let you know that I love you and I always will. That's all I really wanted to tell you. Oh, one more thing, see you soon.
Love,
Samantha, 10

Dear Jesus,

Thank you for everything. Thank you for loving everyone no matter who they are. What is Heaven like? What was your favorite thing to do? What did

it feel like when everyone was mean to You? What is there to do in Heaven? What is it like to be perfect? Where did You live? What is your favorite animal? Thank you for dieing on the cross!
Love,
Kiara, 10

Dear Jesus,

Thank you for all the things you have given me and for all my friends and family. Thank you for being there on hard times and on happy times. There's one question I have allways wanted to ask you, what is heaven like?
Love,
Kent, 10

Dear Jesus,

I want to just ask you one thing. What is your favrite book of the Bible?
Please write back.
Love,
Nick, 10

Dear Jesus,

How are you? Can you answer some questions? How did it feel to walk on water? How did it feel when the soldiers put nails in you? I'm asking you these questions because I am learning about you and what happend. Tell me when I'm in Heaven.
Love,
Daniel, 9

Dear Jesus,

I was woundering when are you coming to get us because it will be hard to die in pain like you did but you rose again. I know if I die the dead will rise first it's a verse in the Bible. I want to know how God was made. It is hard to understand everything but I just want to if what in Heaven because when I go

up with you or die I will know whats in Heaven. Well I will see you one day.
Love,
Jessalyn, 9

Dear Jesus,

I'm thankful for lots of things. I'm thankful for food, animals, nature, a house and car. I'm sure i'm thankful for lots more too. I'm interested in alot to. I'm interested in art, computer, acting and nature. My favorite thing about nature is the animals.
My favorite animals are bunnies, dolphins, butterflies and giraffes. I've studied giraffes before and they are pretty interesting. Thank you Jesus for creating all these things for me to enjoy. See you in heaven someday.
Love,
Madison, 10

Dear Jesus,

I wanted to let you know that I love you so much because you died on the cross for my sins. I think it is amazing that you would give up your life just to save mine. I also wanted to let you know that I'll be watching for you when you come back to earth I love you with all my heart. I wanted to ask a few questions like whats your favorite color. I also wanted to know if God has any parents and what he looks like. I have only one more question to ask. What is your food. I love you.
Madeline, 10

Dear Jesus,

I love you. Someday I will be in heaven with you and god. I can't wait until I can see you face to face.
Love,
Colin

Dear God,

I'm so sorry for all the sins I made. Will you forgive

me? Hope you will forgive me.
Love,
David

Dear Jesus,
Thank you Lord for all you have done for all you have done. Thank you for dying on the cross. I have one question. Why was it that you had to die on the cross and not us?
Love,
Dylan, 9

Dear Jesus,

You died on the cross for are sins! and saved are life! Thank you for my family Lord! And my friends! And thank you for all you done!
Ethan , 7

Dear Jesus

Thank you for dying on the cross for our sins. You saved us all and we thank you for that. We put you first before anything and any prized possession that we have. If you wouldn't die on the cross then none of us would be here today. We love you so much. thanks akgain.
Love,
Reagan, 11

Dear Jesus,

I was wondering when are you coming down from heaven? How was it like on the cross? Was it painful? I realy wan't to go to heaven. I wonder what its like in heaven? You know I love you right. And I know the real reason you were born and why you died it's because you died from my sins, and why you risen to prove your the true king. Easter is not about the candy its about you that resen from the dead.
Love,
Melia, 10
P.S. Please forgive my sins.

Below are letters to Jesus written by teenagers. Most of us remember those years as ever changing while we moved into young adulthood. During this time of life, many things are looming over teens as they pass through high school, thinking about college, or not, wondering what they "will be" when they grow up. This age is filled with new questions not approached as a young girls or boys.

The youth were asked to write to Jesus talking to Him as if He were there with them when they wrote their thoughts. Writing or verbalizing our thoughts can make some questions real, so we will seek answers.

Jesus,
You are known as the Savior, the Son of God, a part of the Trinity, but to me, you are a friend. Being the Son of God entitles you to be all knowing and all powerful, something we as humans will never fully understand. You were perfect while on earth, and you will always be perfect, so in that way, you are my role model. Trying to go through life the way you lived it, by being selfless and spreading the Good News, is a great goal for me.

I've always been brought up in faith. Ever since I can remember, I've learned the classic Bible stories and learned to pray every night before bed. But in the past few years, I've learned that being a Christian is more than reading a Bible or going to Church. Church is not the building; it is the congregation of people, we, the people, ARE the church.

I have been very blessed to have a family that loves me. This blessing is more than what just meets the eye. Yes, I have a mom and a dad that are still happily married, but my family goes much deeper. Many people know the main miracles you have accomplished: turning water into wine or healing the paralytic, but they do not realize the miracles you work today. My life is filled with those miracles. First, I was born 8 weeks premature. To write this letter at 16 with no birth defects, learning disabilities, etc. is a miracle. Next, I am adopted. My birth parents had me when they were teenagers and putting me up for adoption gave me a better life and I know that decision was influenced by you and your Father. Lastly, I am still in contact with my birth family. I see them a few times a year and stay in close contact with them. Being able to be involved in their lives, and knowing they still love and care about me, definitely is a miracle.

So, in writing you this letter, I see how involved you are in my life. Although sometimes I do not understand the path you want me to take, or why you cause me pain, I know that in the long run, the pain will be worth it; because in the end, the victory will triumph over heartache.

I love you and am SO glad I have you in my life. You are my rock, my Savior, and all in all, my friend.
Allie Miller, age 16

Dear Jesus,

Sometimes, I don't understand you.

How you can love me? how you can overlook all my faults? and call me, your beautiful creation, made in your image? I don't get it. I don't get how you aren't ashamed of me. How you can love me the same yesterday, today and tomorrow..? though I'm probably worse off one day to the next. How can you always be there for me? How can you have your arms wide open? how can you listen to everything that I have to say? Though I don't give you the same respect? How can you be everything that I am not? I want so very badly to be faithful to you. I want to serve you, and you only. I want to be able to keep my eyes on you. Without wavering.

I want to focus on you, in tough times, not my problems, that are really so small, why do I make this bigger than it has to be? You have the whole world, you have me... in your hands, but I choose to focus on the little things that bring me down, instead.
I don't understand it.

Why do you choose to love me? Despite all I've done? There are so many things that I don't understand about you. And what makes it even more confusing is that, you don't need me to understand it.
You aren't a fairy. You won't disappear, if people cease to believe in you. You are God. Creator of everything. And you don't need me. You don't need my belief, or understanding. You don't even need my praise.
It doesn't make any sense, why is it, though you don't need my praise, or my belief, you give me the privilege to do so? Is praising, and believing in you, for your benefit, or mine? I guess that's another thing I'll never know.

But one thing I do know is this.

I do believe in you.
I do love you.
I do need you. More than I could ever express. You're the best thing that's ever happened to me. And though I don't know all that much about you and I'll have to wait awhile to find out. I still choose to believe that you are God. I still choose to love you. And I know, without a doubt, that you love me back. And through the power that I'm given from you. You believe in me too.

You have given me, through you: Faith to move mountains, love to cast out fear, light to shine in the darkness. You have given me the world, and every chance to excel.

So I won't let the unknown bring me down, I won't let it affect my relationship with you. I love you. And through you, I can face this big world, and all the things that try to bring me down.

So Jesus, thank you, for always loving me, thank you, for never giving up on me. Thank you for giving me the desire to know more about you, and the understanding that I might have to wait awhile to get the answers to my questions. Thank you for giving your

son, for me, and many, many others. Thank you, for creating me in your image, and thank you. Most of all. For your love. Your perfect love, it's through that love that I have the hope and strength to go on.
Love,
Your daughter in Christ, Tamara, 15
Dear Jesus,

If I were five, I would ask you why you make it rain. If I were eight, I would ask you why the Bible is so big. But now that I am 13, I have some more complex questions for you. Like why do I have such a hard time trying to spread your word to others and why is it so hard to obey all of your commands. I have learned the 10 commandments and studied your word, but the world we live in today is so much different from the one that you lived in. However, I do want to say that I am glad to be talking to you. First, you were my best friend when others were not. I could have my own conversations with you at night when my day was bad or good, and without verbally speaking, it still felt like you were talking back. Jesus, you have known me all of my life. We have shared all of the good and bad moments. You know every thought that I have ever had. You know exactly what will happen to me in the future. And I pray that your Will will be done.

I also would like to ask you a few favors. I wish that you would help guide me down the path that you would like me to go on. As I grow up, I begin to think more and more about who I will be. As you already know, I have a lot of options, but I hope that you will help me choose the right one. Also I ask you to do what is best for my friends, family and everybody else in the world.

I have been focusing on things that are about me and what I want, but now I just want to thank you. I want to thank you for giving me an amazing family. Not only an amazing family at home, but my church family as well. I also wish to thank you for my friends, because they are amazing and they not only are easy to talk to, but along with my family, they make my days wonderful. In addition, I would like to thank you for the people who spend hours helping other people. For example, Samaritan's Purse and everyone else who helps to lead service projects like those. Lastly, I would like to thank you for your missionaries, and all of those who are helping me continue my walk with you.

Lord Jesus, my leader and Savior, as we end this conversation, I ask that you continue to watch over me, and keep me on the path that you want me to be on.
Your loving Daughter,
Kristina, 13

Dear Jesus,

For the past one year and two months, You have been the greatest thing to always keep me going. When I think about all You did, it just bewilders me. I am amazed by how powerful and truly great You are. When times are rough, I know that You will always be there for me when I feel like nobody else will. You continue to hold me up and keep me strong since the passing of my Dad on September 22, 2008; You continue to be my rock when situations at school are not right. I will always stand up and praise You when everything is fabulous. You have taught me how to keep my temper when in the inside I'm screaming for Your assistance. The presence of You and the guidance You have showed me have led me to the person I am today.

Things are not going that great, as You know. School is not so peachy, family issues are doleful and "friends" are trying to lead me astray. See, in the school I go to, the few people that actually believe in Your great and true word are not really my friends. They think I'm weird and different by the way I act and look, and so nobody really talks to me. On the other side, the majority of the other kids in my school don't share the concept what a real Christian is. All of them do not believe and some don't even care. That is my main challenge right now. I have a year and a half before I'm off to college, but to get through this next year and a half, these people are always going to be around me. Sure, they are occasionally nice, but in the dark times, they lead me to asking "Why would You put me through this?" or "Why can't You do something about this to make me happier?" When I am reading the Bible by myself, I know that it is Your will and You know what is right for me. But, I still ask for You to show me the way, to show me how to work in their lives so they can maybe see how great You are someday.

Despite the people at school, I do have an excellent core support system found in my band teacher and his wife, my church, my homeschooled friends, and my youth group. They keep me seeing You and show me how great, true, and eternal You are. They are definitely the greatest blessing You have ever given me. I just could never thank You enough for leading them to me. They make me want to become an even better Christian. They challenge me in my everyday life to have You shining through me, and, believe me, that is something I will constantly struggle with.
Jesus, I just ask You to continue to help me. Show me that everything is in Your will and that You have an amazing plan for me. Continue to work in my life to lead me to that one moment that it will all be worth it. Thank You so much for dying for my sins so I can have eternal life in Heaven. That is the greatest present that could ever be given.
Keep watching over Adam for our community! Also, say hi to my daddy, grandparents, and Jeremiah please, too!
Love,
Beth Nesser, 16

Dear Jesus,

I am 16 now and you have helped me so much. I pray to you all the time and thank you for loving me no matter what. I am scared about my future

and hope to be successful like my brother. I know I do well in sports but still struggle in school. I have grown up without a father and my Mom has done her best to keep good role models in my life. I know I can always count on you to guide me. My brother is 12 years older and I count on him a lot for advice even though he lives far away. I hope to keep my life with you as the center of all I do. With you beside me, I will be ok.
Cameron, 16

Jesus,

I know I'm not the great Christian I can be. I don't go to church every Sunday and the only service I do is helping with a program at my church every Thursday. My schedule is very packed and sometimes, things much less important than you crowd out my time with you. But I know your love and how great it is. I know that you gave your own life for mine, so that I may be free from my sins.

Jesus, sometimes I feel like high school is Noah's Ark. Everybody has their pair. Every girl has a best friend that she always hangs out with. I don't have just one person I hang out with. I'm just close friends with many people. Sometimes I feel like I don't have a pair and everybody else does. But I'm happy and I'm okay with that. Is that okay or is it strange that I don't have one certain person I hang out with?

A lot of kids at my school are into bad things. They do drugs; get drunk, and many other things. I disagree strongly with doing things like this. Also, I study a lot and try my best to get good grades. My friends and I don't do the things many other girls do so we seem to stick out of the crowd. Is it better to stand out and be firm in what I believe in or to step down slightly and blend in with the others? Is blending in really that bad?

Most kids my age already know what they want to be when they grow up. Me, on the other hand, I have no idea what I want to be when I grow up. This weekend, I went to an overnighter at my church for high school students. We talked about the true meaning of Christmas and all that comes with it. I had a great time and knew most of the information we were learning about. Everything was easy for me until I had to write a letter to God. We were instructed to tell or ask God anything we wanted but we should probably include something about letting God have control of our lives. I sat there, blankly staring at the piece of paper for a few minutes. If I have no plan for the future, how am I not already putting my future in God's hands? While I was sitting there listening to the soothing music and watching everybody else in the room write; I realized that I really should ask God about my future. So Jesus, I will do whatever you believe is best for me. What do you think I am best suited for? How can I serve you better in my future?

Beauty is everywhere I look. It's hard for me to believe that everything on this earth was created in six days. But that just shows me how powerful God is and his capability to create amazing miracles when nobody expects them. As I stare out my window now, out into the powdery, white snow, I am in a state of total peace. Looking at the world and its beauty puts me in this peaceful state. That is how amazing you truly are, Jesus. When I think of you, my mind is calm and I am overwhelmed by the sudden peace that flies over my body and mind. Thank you for giving me peace.

Jesus, thank you for always forgiving me when I do something wrong. Please help me to be the best Christian I can and to not sin as much as I do now without noticing. How can I show the world your great love? How can you use me to show the world your love and everything that comes with it? Life is hard and sometimes it seems like it would be easier if Earth were just like Heaven. Although I know how hard life is, I understand that it is just a test everybody has to take to get into Heaven. Please help me to be the best person I can be on Earth so that I may pass the test and be able to have eternal life. Thank you

for always being there for me and carrying me when I couldn't walk on my own. If only everybody knew your love; the world would be perfect. Thank you for always showing me your love.
Love always,
Your servant, Melissa Kauffman, 14
Dear Jesus,

Remember when I was younger, how I always asked Mom for a little brother or sister? I never thought it'd happen like this.

What a story my life has been so far; you've taken and given, but never left me waiting for very long.
It wasn't too many years ago that you gave and took away the precious little boy that was gone before he lived. We had built up so much hope and excitement, and then it was gone in the blink of an eye. All the thrilling thoughts of a little brother that had been passing through my mind again and again were torn to pieces. Of course, being so young, I couldn't quite understand fully what had happened; I just knew that I wasn't getting a brother and it hurt. A few years passed by, painful yet hopeful for something in the future. I still wanted a sibling. I wanted the house to not be so quiet all the time; I wanted a real little baby to hold instead of the plastic dolls I had.
But it was your plan all along; here comes the good part when you make all my dreams come true, remember?

We got matched up with an African American mother from an adoption agency. It was going to be a girl. Yay! Oh I couldn't wait to dress her up in adorable clothes and carry her around and brag on God's beautiful gift.

Soon the day came for the baby to be born. We got a call from the mother who was in the hospital ready to go into labor. We drove two hours to the city she was in and met her in the hospital room; she hadn't had the baby yet. What a shock it was when the nurse said, "Do you think it'll be a boy or a girl?" We thought for sure it was going to be a girl! We'd gotten

all pink things for the baby already. To our surprise, out came a little boy; but really, whether it was a boy or girl, it didn't matter at all because we had a baby, I had a sibling. My new brother; an adorable, light brown baby. He was perfect. After a few days of staying in our city's hospital for adoption reasons, we took him home.
Now, three years later, he is still wonderful. Although the terrible two's (and three's) are definitely terrible, I wouldn't trade it for anything. I love that little boy with all my heart.

Jesus, you are amazing. You open doors, sometimes close them abruptly, but always open another one. You keep us on our toes, but let us rest in your reassurance.

Thank you for every single blessing and all the hardships, because when they are through, we see your perfection in everything.
Love,
Gwendolyn Schillinger, 14

During each stage of our lives we can look back to see where we have been. These letters by children and youth make me think about the time of my life when I was a child or teen. These letters also confirm that our youth shows hope for this nation and world. The news tells us plenty of negative information and stories, and the good in this world is often missing. My hope is that you are as encouraged and blessed by reading these letters as I am.

God nudged me as I was working on this chapter. He told me it was not yet complete. One name came to mind immediately. I called Ruth hoping she would dictate a letter to Jesus that I could use to close this chapter. I am glad I had my pen in hand and a pad of paper ready because she did not hesitate.

Dear Jesus,

I have had such a wonderful life and am glad to have a chance to give thanks to you. There is so much beauty in life, and I want young people see that. I never stopped to say this before. Life goes so fast, and we take it for granted. We're so busy with our trials and tribulations; we don't take the time *to thank you like we should.*

I'd like to send a wakeup call to young people today who get so involved in life—all the electronics and gadgets that take their attention away from what is important in life. I know it's been said often that the best things in life are free—but it's true, believe me. The air, water, time—so much is free in this life that we don't recognize. I fear we are losing the things that matter most in this life. We have too many distractions and temptations that take us away from the things that matter.

I'm thankful for my friends who have stood by my side all these years; for my church and church family where I can worship freely without fear of retaliation by anyone; for family. But most of all I'm thankful for you, Jesus. My Savior. Without you, what would this life mean? Christmas would be hollow with just be lights and shopping for show and no meaning. I can't imagine life without you in the center, dear Jesus.

At ninety-five and a half, I'm so blessed, unworthy, and guilty because I have taken things for granted. I'm so grateful and don't know what you are saving me for (I'm still here), but I hope I fulfill whatever it is. When I see a person who can't walk or talk, I thank God He has allowed me to keep most of my physical abilities. True, I have a pacemaker, but I also have a Maker who knows the number of my days. Yes, I have hearing aids because my ears are weak. But I pray I always hear your voice, Jesus, and that my heart is always focused on you, no matter how I spend my days.

Thank you for all the blessings I can count when looking back over my life and around me today.
Love,
Ruth Sawyer Jividen, 95 ½

Ruth holds a special place in my heart as I have become friends with her in the last few years. Together, we did a series of stories for the local newspaper called "Ruth Remembers." She is the last descendent of the first settler in Grove City, Ohio. Her memory is huge and vivid. Many people have enjoyed reading her experiences of growing up in the early 1900's. Ruth is a bright light in the lives of many, showing God's love in all she does and says.

Another woman I have gotten to know at our Ladies Bible Study is Mary. Her faith is deep and she was eager to share a letter to Jesus.

Dear Jesus,

I come to you today to thank you for being my guiding hand all my life. When I was five years old, my mother became sick and was not able to care for me and my two sisters and brother. We were placed in a county orphanage for two and a half years. This orphanage was not a very good orphanage. My father's pastor told him to put us in a Lutheran orphanage in Loysville, Pennsylvania. He told my father that this was a good, Christian Orphanage with 320 children in it. I know you know all this as you gave a helping hand financially to keep the orphanage to take care of so many children that became good Christian children.

We had church service every day and that helped us learn and do our daily tasks such as cleaning our bedrooms, sewing, mending and other duties. We had our own church and school. We were very well disciplined. I graduated in 1938. My mother died when I was 16 years old. I only saw her twice before her death. I was 19 years old one week before I graduated. You usually had to leave the orphanage at the age of 18 but they let me stay to graduate. I never saw my father after that. He died when he was 59 years old of leukemia.

My family in Myerstown, Pennsylvania wanted me to come live with them and to let me go to Beauty School to become a beautician. I worked in a beauty shop for about six years. I met my first husband in a movie theater. He was a soldier in the Army. I stayed with his family in St. Louis, Il-

linois until he got out of the Army and then we got married. I was unable to carry my beautician license in Illinois so I got a job sewing in St. Louis, Missouri, across the Mississippi River.
We had two lovely daughters and moved to Wisconsin as he got a job there working on trains as a fireman.

Jesus, as you know, we bought our first house and lived there for four months and then my husband died. He died from smoking and drinking. I stayed living in the home for about 11 years. I lost my first born daughter when she was 54 years old. Jesus, as you know, I had some rough times through the years.

I met my second husband, Bill, in the same apartment building where I lived in 1994. We kept meeting each other by the mail boxes. We married in 1995. He died at the age of 92 of pneumonia. I now live with my second born daughter and son-in-law in Ohio. After my husband passed away February 2009, they came to Wisconsin and packed my belongins and moved me to Ohio to live with them. My daughter told me the role has now reversed; she will now take care of me.

I just want to thank you for being my guiding hand all my life. We belong to a wonderful WELS (Wisconsin Evangelical Lutheran Synod) Christian Lutheran church call Beautiful Savior Lutheran Church. My daughter and her husband are a wonderful blessing to me. Thank you for them. Thank you Jesus for all your help and blessings through the years.

Jesus, I am now 91 (2011) years old and pray I will meet you soon in heaven.
Mary V. Reuter

In your struggle against sin, you have not yet resisted to the point of shedding your blood. And have you completely forgotten this word of encouragement that addresses you as a father addresses his son? It says, "My son, do not make light of the Lord's discipline, and do not lose heart when he rebukes you, because the Lord disciplines the one he loves, and he chastens everyone he accepts as his son." Endure hardship as discipline; God is treating you as his children. For what children are not disciplined by their father? If you are not disciplined—and everyone undergoes discipline—then you are not legitimate, not true sons and daughters at all. Moreover, we have all had human fathers who disciplined us and we respected them for it. How much more should we submit to the Father of spirits and live! They disciplined us for a little while as they thought best; but God disciplines us for our good, in order that we may share in his holiness. No discipline seems pleasant at the time, but painful. Later on, however, it produces a harvest of righteousness and peace for those who have been trained by it.

Therefore, strengthen your feeble arms and weak knees. "Make level paths for your feet," so that the lame may not be disabled, but rather healed.

-Hebrews 12:4-13

5

Jesus Our Shepherd

Our valleys may be filled with foes and tears; but we can lift our eyes to the hills to see God and the angels, heaven's spectators, who support us according to God's infinite wisdom as they prepare our welcome home.
-Billy Graham[49]

One day in church, people were lined up to receive communion. In this particular church, people would walk forward and kneel at a railing while the pastor gave them the bread and wine. I noticed a gray-haired woman in this line who must have been the grandmother of a baby she held in her arms. The child's dark hair was standing straight up in the air, and his large brown eyes were wide with wonder as he peered over his grandmother's shoulder. Behind them stood a younger woman with long, brown hair who I knew was the mother by simply watching them. The grandmother was gently rocking the baby back and forth, and I noticed the younger woman was rocking in the same way, at the same time as the woman holding the baby. She was also leaning toward the baby's face as if silently communicating to the baby that Mama was near. It was a sweet and soothing action to watch. I found myself smiling and wondering if they realized they were rocking in rhythm as dancers would.

Christ is like that with us. He is always watching and silently communicating with each of us. He is also moving with us—behind us and next to us. Many times, He is holding us like the grandmother held the baby. He is ever-present in our lives even if we don't realize it or take the time to know His presence.

---

49   See Appendix: Quote References

Psalm 23

This Psalm was my only memory verse as a girl. Although I didn't always understand the meaning, the words have been in my head and heart most of my life. You have probably experienced reading something and then, years later, reading it again only to find a new meaning. Reading the Bible is like that for me. When I read a Bible verse again after some time has passed, the meaning becomes so clear, even though before the verse seemed to be simply words.

As I go to sleep, I pray. If my brain is easily distracted, I say the Lord's Prayer to keep me focused. Sometimes I sing it silently in my head; other times, I use American Sign Language in my head. This prayer is how Jesus taught us to pray.

> *This, then, is how you should pray: "Our Father in heaven, hallowed be your name, your kingdom come, your will be done, on earth as it is in heaven. Give us today our daily bread. And forgive us our debts, as we also have forgiven our debtors. And lead us not into temptation, but deliver us from the evil one." For if you forgive other people when they sin against you, your heavenly Father will also forgive you. But if you do not forgive others their sins, your Father will not forgive your sins.*
> *-Matthew 6:9-15*

One evening, as I was praying, I couldn't focus. I started to recite Psalm 23 in my mind, but realized I couldn't remember all of it, at least not in complete order. It troubled me that memorization, and remembering Scripture, has become difficult for me. In a Bible study, when I voiced this concern, a woman named Lorie said that the Bible tells us to keep the Word in our hearts. She went on to say that it doesn't matter if we can't recite the Bible verses as long as we hold them in our heart. The next day, I picked up my Bible to read the Psalm again. It was like a balm.

> The LORD is my shepherd; I lack nothing.
> He makes me lie down in green pastures.
> He leads me beside quiet waters.
> He refreshes my soul.
> He guides me along the right paths for his name's sake.
> Even though I walk through the darkest valley, I will fear no evil,
> for you are with me; your rod and your staff, they comfort me.
> You prepare a table before me in the presence of my enemies.
> You anoint my head with oil; my cup overflows.

Surely your goodness and love will follow me all the days of my life,
and I will dwell in the house of the LORD forever.

The more I learn about Jesus and His role as our Shepherd, the more I love this Psalm. I was always confused about how a rod and staff could comfort me. Time has shown me that the rod, the discipline and authority of God, is a good thing. The rod is used by shepherds for counting, guiding, rescuing, and protecting sheep. I want to be counted, guided, rescued, and protected by Jesus, my Shepherd, don't you? This is truly comforting and reassuring. On the other hand, the staff is an instrument of support. Therefore, Jesus uses His rod and staff to comfort us all while He supports us, counts us as one of His sheep, guides us on the narrow path, rescues us from our sinful nature, and protects us from the evil in this world.

Part of a song I wrote, called "Made with Love," shows that I was thinking on this years ago.

He calls with His sweet, gentle voice; you know you must obey.
Made with love, made with love,
We as His sheep should run to Him and let Him know we hear![50]

Sheep hear the shepherd's voice. He guides them to water, pastures, and safety; it's no wonder the sheep listen. It is said the sheep know their shepherd's voice, and the Bible confirms this fact, saying,

When he has brought out all his own, he goes on ahead of them, and his sheep follow him because they know his voice
-John 10:4

What do you think? If a man owns a hundred sheep, and one of them wanders away, will he not leave the ninety-nine on the hills and go to look for the one that wandered off?
-Matthew 18:12

We aren't sheep in the literal sense, naturally, but we have a Shepherd who will lead us and "makes (us) lie down in green pastures. He leads (us) beside quiet waters. He restores (our) soul. He guides (us) along the right paths."
Phillip Keller writes in his books, *A Shepherd Looks at Psalm 23*

---

50   See Appendix: Quote References

and *A Shepherd Looks at the Good Shepherd and His Sheep,* details about shepherding. He describes the rod as a tool the shepherds hone to fit their hands specifically and use to protect their sheep while in the fields. When a sheep nears danger and out of the shepherd's reach, it is not uncommon for the shepherd to hurl his rod at the sheep to warn the lamb of danger they may not see. Though this may seem cruel, the shepherd loves the lamb so much that he's willing to do temporary injury to keep it from certain death. This same shepherd will carry the injured lamb until it is well, just as Jesus carries us when we are injured spiritually.

God's Word is the rod that protects us as we go through our days. Jesus calls to us throughout our day, and we need to be aware of His voice that protects and guides us to do His will.

Savior, Like a Shepherd[51]

> Savior, like a shepherd lead us, much we need Thy tender care;
> In Thy pleasant pastures feed us, for our use Thy folds prepare.
> Blessed Jesus, blessed Jesus! Thou hast bought us, Thine we are.
> Blessed Jesus, blessed Jesus! Thou hast bought us, Thine we are.
> We are Thine, do Thou befriend us, be the guardian of our way;
> Keep Thy flock, from sin defend us, seek us when we go astray.
> Blessed Jesus, blessed Jesus! Hear, O hear us when we pray.
> Blessed Jesus, blessed Jesus! Hear, O hear us when we pray.
> Thou hast promised to receive us, poor and sinful though we be;
> Thou hast mercy to relieve us, grace to cleanse and power to free.
> Blessed Jesus, blessed Jesus! Let us early turn to Thee.
> Blessed Jesus, blessed Jesus! Let us early turn to Thee.
> Early let us seek Thy favor, early let us do Thy will;
> Blessed Lord and only Savior, with Thy love our bosoms fill.
> Blessed Jesus, blessed Jesus! Thou hast loved us, love us still.
> Blessed Jesus, blessed Jesus! Thou hast loved us, love us still.

Jesus has many names in the Bible. Too many to list here. After a search on the Internet, I found a helpful website. Some of my favorites include Almighty, Alpha and Omega, Bright and Morning Star, Counselor, Everlasting Father, Lamb of God, Savior and True Vine.

---

51   See Appendix: Music Notes

6

Warts and All, He Still Loves Us

God sees with utter clarity who we are. He is undeceived as to our warts and wickedness. But when God looks at us that is not all he sees. He also sees who we are intended to be, who we will one day become.
-John Ortberg[52]

WE ARE ALL PUMPKINS AFTER ALL...

A woman was asked by a coworker, "What is it like to be a Christian?"

The coworker replied, "It's like being a pumpkin. God picks you from the patch, brings you in, and washes all the dirt off you. Then He cuts off the top and scoops out all the yucky stuff. He removes the seeds of doubt, hate, and greed. Then He carves you a new smiling face and puts His light inside of you to shine for all the world to see."

We are all pumpkins with yucky stuff inside. God has done remarkable things in us, and we want the pumpkin patch to be large and growing. One way we can push potential pumpkins away is by using words that seem oppressive, judgmental, or "preachy" when we talk. God wants us to share His love in all we do. The topic of "churchy" words came up in a Sunday school class I attended. When I began studying these words, using a Bible concordance and a thesaurus, I realized that I did not understand the true meaning of many of the words I had heard for years.

These words should get us thinking about how we use lan-

See Appendix: Quote References

guage to shepherd people or to push them away. As a person who became deaf and had to learn American Sign Language, I learned about our body language (what we say without uttering one word) and that, in sign language, not every word signed is used to make a point. For example, in English, we might say, "Look at that man over there with the long stringy hair. What is he doing here?" Yet in sign language, the main words used would translate into English as, "There, man, hair (indicating not nice). Here? Why?" The message is the same, but no one had to whisper. God heard our meaning in both situations. We must take care to not judge by appearances—actually not to judge at all. As humans, we tend to look at a person and "size them up." God sees our heart with and without the warts and yucky stuff.

The Bible tells us in 1 Samuel 16:7, "The LORD does not look at the things people look at. People look at the outward appearance, but the LORD looks at the heart" and in 2 Timothy 2:19, "Nevertheless, God's solid foundation stands firm, sealed with this inscription: 'The Lord knows those who are his,' and, 'Everyone who confesses the name of the Lord must turn away from wickedness.'" No matter what our outward appearance, God knows our hearts and minds.

Without realizing it, Christians, like any close-knit group, can tend to form cliques, an exclusive circle of people with a common purpose. We gravitate toward one another because it is comfortable. But it's important that we see those who are new or visiting. Though we don't know every person walking through the church doors, we need to meet them where they are, whether they look like "church people" or not. We should especially reach out to them if they look or act out of place.

Even those who have been a part of a church for some time may feel left out. I was in a Sunday school class listening to the teacher when the entire group of women starting holding up their fingers, one at a time, saying something as they raised each finger. I had been in this class for months, but I was at a loss. A strange bout of self-consciousness overtook me as I looked around and realized I was the only one who did not know this list; I really felt outside the group for the first time. Not being shy, I asked what they had said. The motions were from a study they had done, and they repeated it for me: "1. God is who He says He is, 2. God can do what He says He can do, 3. I am who God says I am, 4. I can do all through Christ, 5. God's word is alive and active in me." Then I was told one woman, Joy, had added number six:"Jesus paid it all, and when I choose to follow Him, I am forgiven.", while pointing to the palm of her hand, indicating the nail. Beautiful.

Warts and All, He Still Loves Us

The teacher sent me the list, and I printed it out. I know in my heart that these women, my friends, were not trying to exclude me or anyone else, but from this experience, and many others through the years, I have a heart for the stranger or newcomer. I wonder, if I had been a visitor, would this have sent me away? We never know what can affect others' decisions about church. For this reason, I feel strongly that we all need to be aware of things like this in order to teach and share with everyone.

Whenever we moved and sought out a new church to attend, we often knew quickly if the church was one we wanted to visit again. Genuine friendliness has been important in our choices, but not the only factor. Let's do a little imagining of what it would like to visit your church for the first time. Place yourself in this fictional person's place for a few minutes. Would your experience be similar to this next story?

Imagine you are attending church for the first time in your life. You walk in the doors of a nearby church and are greeted profusely by someone handing you some paper. They ask if you are new and what your name is, but all you want to know is where the show is taking place.

You wander rather aimlessly following voices or music, hoping you will know what to do when you arrive in this place. You sit, read the paper you were given which you realize later is called a bulletin. You see numbers, names, topics, lists of meetings, and what is called something like Order of Service. The music begins again and everyone stands—so you do, too. You feel self-conscious and hope you figure out what is happening.

You sing along, after you found the songbook or as you strain to read the screen at the front of the room. After all, you sat in the very back because you want to leave unnoticed.

Now everyone is lowering their heads while one person talks. Everyone sits, and so do you.

It goes on like this for a little while, but just when you are getting the hang of it, something changes. What is that thing those men are passing down the rows of people? It looks like food, and you think it's odd to feed people in this manner. You quickly look at the bulletin to see it's called the Lord's Supper.

Now you're really panicked. What in the world is that? And what do you do? Then you notice someone next to you gently poking your arm, and you look at him. He is pointing to some words in his bulletin, and you scan it fast. The man with the food is coming closer to your row. Sweat breaks out on your forehead, and you feel dizzy. As you scan the stranger's bulletin where he is pointing, you sigh with relief. You have heard of communion but not the Lord's Supper.

The stranger whispers in your ear, "If you have accepted Christ as your Savior, you are welcome to take part in this meal." Meal? The cup is so tiny and the bread has been broken into bite-size pieces. You smile at the stranger and try to catch your breath.

Here it comes—a plate with bread. Your hands shake as you take it, but as something makes you think, "I think I'll pass," you give it to the stranger next to you. Here comes a metal dish with tiny cups of what looks like grape juice. The plate rattles as you take it, and you think everyone is looking right at you. The man who handed the plate to you gently touches your shoulder and whispers, "My name is Jim. I'll explain this to you later. Pass it on." He smiles as if he knows your thoughts. You nod a thank you and pass the plate. You notice your hand is no longer shaking. Jim moves to the next row. After this is completed, Jim comes back to you and asks the stranger next to you to move over. Now Jim is sitting on your left where the stranger had been.

He doesn't say a word but quietly guides you through the rest of the service with a nod or a smile using his pen to draw arrows and circles to show where they are in the service. You breathe easier, look at Jim, and smile. You think he looks familiar somehow. You shake your head and listen to what the man is saying in what is called a sermon.

People are opening books when the man up front asks them to turn to some book in their Bibles. You figure they each have their own Bibles and are following along. You have heard about Bibles but never held one in your hands. Why is that, you ponder?

Here they go, standing again and singing. Some people are holding their hands in the air. Are they asking questions or trying to get someone's attention? It's so foreign to you, but for some reason, it feels good. These people seem happy, even content. Someone behind you sure can't sing, but she is bellowing out the words with gusto.

Now everyone is hugging and talking. It must be over. Just when you think, "What now?" Jim taps your shoulder and gives his name again. He doesn't ask you anything at all, but you find yourself giving your name and smiling. You start talking like you've know Jim for years, and you feel relieved because you feel connected somehow. This man is nice and not pushy, even accepting. He knows you are new, certainly. Now you are the stranger. Jim asks if you have a few minutes, and you say you do. He then says, "I'd like to introduce you to my family. This is my wife, Mary, and my daughter Libby and her son, Tony." You shake hands with each, and you notice they are all smiling and that Tony is looking up at you. You look at the boy and smile. He says, "Hey mister, you're new, aren't you?" He doesn't wait for an answer and adds, "I hate being new. I never know what to do."

You smile again and reply, "Yes, I'm new. Never been in a church before, but I've driven by this church for months and decided to visit."

Jim and Mary give each other a look, and Mary says, "We're going to lunch at a place down the road. We'd love to have you come as our guest. I won't take no for an answer, unless you need to be somewhere else."

You hesitate, and Tony says, "They have great cheeseburgers. Do you play baseball? Our team is undefeated so far." You are completely caught by surprise because you played in Little League as a boy. "Tony, will you tell me about it if I go to lunch?" He nods and smiles. You thank them for the invite, and you follow them to the restaurant.

Children are the ultimate icebreakers.

This is one possible scenario that can take place in any church, on any given Sunday. This one had a good outcome, but there are other scenes happening everyday which aren't as positive. As I stated above, we humans tend to size a person up with the first look. It's not fair, of course, but most of us do it anyway. Here is another church scene; do you recognize yourself in it? It's not a test, and there will be no quiz. I confess that I too have made judgments by appearance only or by a comment made by someone or an action I witnessed. By writing this scene, it is healing for me as I see how far God has brought me away from this type of thinking. I'm richer for it, and I like living in my skin more since the plank of unfair judgment in my eye was removed.

"What a beautiful morning it is!" the pastor says as he greets you at the door of the church.

"It's a little hot, but pretty," you reply, wishing you'd stayed home to read the paper and drink another cup of coffee on this hot summer day. But you want to do your duty.

The greeters are buzzing around and talking to some people you've never met. You opt to take a trip to the restroom because you're not feeling very social today. As you lean down to drink from the water fountain, you see a woman come in the side door. You realize your mouth is hanging open, but you aren't drinking the water. You are staring at Penelope Rivers.

"How dare she step into our church!" you think. "Such a hussy. She thinks she's such hot stuff. Her with her tattoos." You wonder how to avoid seeing her.

Then it happens. She sees you. Ouch.

You put on a smile, knowing it doesn't reach your eyes, and say, "Well, Penelope, what brings you to church?" as you emphasize the word church hoping she gets the subtle message.

She does. As she walks past you, she gives you a half smile and keeps walking. The greeters hand her a bulletin, and they smile and welcome her. What's their problem? Don't they know "about her"? How could they be happy to see her?

You are completely puzzled. Disappointed.

Then several teens walk up to Penelope and say, "Cool tattoo! Where did you get it?"

Penelope smiles and says, "I got it years ago. I was about your age and can't remember where."

"I want one, too, but my parents say no way," a teen girl says.

As you stand just out of sight of Penelope, you are surprised at her response.

"Listen to your parents, girl. I wish I had. You know the Bible even says we aren't to mar our bodies with things like tattoos. Did you know that?"

"No way! Where does it say that?"

You just know she doesn't have the answer, or at least hope she doesn't. Does the Bible really say anything about it?

"Well, it's in Leviticus 19:28 which says, 'Do not cut your bodies for the dead or put tattoo marks on yourselves. I am the LORD.' Look it up if you don't believe me, but it's one I learned a few years back, and it stuck with me."

You are shocked by what Penelope had to say and guilt washes over you like a river.

"Let me ask you something, kids. When I walked through the doors of this church this morning, do you think my appearance put people off, or do you think everyone feels comfortable talking to me? Think about it. Believe me, if I could start again, I'd never get these tattoos, but getting rid of them costs more than I can pay."

The teens listened and then asked her some more questions. These same youth didn't listen when you talked to them, but they listened to Penelope. What gives?

The music starts, and everyone heads to the worship center when she spots you again.

"Hey kids, one more thing, OK?" she said. They all turned to her and smiled, listening—again.

"There's one more verse I want you all to look up. It's Romans 14:13. It goes something like this: 'Therefore let us stop passing judgment on one another. Instead, make up your mind not to put any stumbling block or obstacle in the way of your brother or sister.' If I'm stopping someone from thinking I'm a Christian because of these tattoos, I'm really sorry. But think about it before you go marking up your body, OK? Promise me?"

They all give her a thumbs up, and you notice Penelope put her arm gently around one of the girl's shoulders. The girl grins up at her and sits in the same row of seats as her. You see her whisper something in Penelope's ear and point at her Mom.

Now you're flustered and appalled—at yourself. "I was judging her! I had no right, and I knew it. What should I do now?"

Right then, the pastor stands up front. You realize you're still standing in the aisle and scurry to a seat nearby.

"Let us pray," the pastor said as you bow your head. "Dear Lord, as we enter into a time of worship today, help us to see you first and to see each other as you see us—as sinners who are forgiven. Help us to turn to you when we are confused and seek your guidance because we know, when we ask you to help us, you will answer. In Jesus' name we pray, amen."

Your head stays bowed. Tears come to your eyes, and you know what God was telling you to do. No more hiding. Fear dissipated, and the service ended with everyone singing, "Make Me a Blessing." You smiled knowing that God is still talking, and you are still listening.

You turn and wait for Penelope who is sitting a few rows ahead of you. The young girl is talking to her again and has apparently introduced her Mom to Penelope, and the women are having an animated conversation with lots of laughter. You find you are chuckling quietly.

"Penelope? Can we talk a minute?" you ask quietly as everyone left the worship service.

"Sure. What's up?"

"Do you have plans for lunch? I know of a cute cafe that serves great sandwiches. Want to join me?"

Her brow furrows only briefly, and then she grins, showing light in her eyes.

"Why sure! Sounds great! Tell me where it is, and we'll meet there."

"Follow me," you say while blushing. Follow me? God sure is working on you. Anticipation finds you. For once, you let God show you the way, and you know it's you who is going to change, not Penelope.

Thank God.

Here the main character was nudged into action, but first God turned on a light in her heart. What she saw shocked her. I've been there, haven't you? It might not have been tattoos or anything like it, but you and God remember. That's enough. We need to let that light shine in our darkness, so we aren't trying to hide. Jesus is calling you out of your hiding place just like when we played hide-and-seek as children and the seeker "gave up" calling "Olly, olly oxen free!" You jump out of your hiding place, and you are free. You run to home base, meet up with your friends and go on playing other games. Had you stayed hidden, the feeling of being called to freedom would have been lost.

Come out of your hiding place, let the light shine on your life, and share the joy with others. While doing that, remember how lonely it was to be hiding, all alone, in the dark, before you answered the call to freedom.

Few things are more infectious than a godly lifestyle. The people you rub shoulders with everyday need that kind of challenge. Not prudish. Not preachy. Just cracker jack clean living. Just honest to goodness, bone-deep, non-hypocritical integrity.
-Charles Swindoll[53]

CHURCH WORDS

When I began this section, I was thinking that what have been called "churchy" words in some communities are actually comforting for me to hear. Some words are symbolic and hold meaning in the validation or familiarity of meaning. It is my responsibility to learn what they mean. But it can be embarrassing not knowing the meanings of words you have heard or used for many years. It reminds me of people whose names often escape me, and I get tired of asking them to repeat their names over and over again. When this happens, I don't use their names. Knowing the definitions of the words used in many church services helps with our understanding, but I have learned that understanding with our hearts is equally important and ultimately more meaningful.

Thinking back fondly on my days growing up in the Church of Messiah, United Methodist Church in Westerville, Ohio, good memories abound. We lived a little more than a block from church. As I recall, the church bell rang loudly as a reminder that Sunday school would begin soon. The next ringing told us that church was about to begin. I loved being wakened by the sound of the old, clanging bell. As early as I can remember, I was in choir at church. We

---

53   See Appendix: Quote References

always wore robes. As a girl, we wore robes that were white with big red bows at our necks. As a teen and on into adulthood, we wore silky robes with straight, long scarf-like cloth over our shoulders and down the front of our robes. We lined up in the narthex, or outside the back of the sanctuary where services were held, and walked in unison, holding our music folders up. As we walked, we sang, "Holy, Holy, Holy" or a similar song. Our steps were in time with the beat. Now that memory is sweet to me even though we did the same thing each week. I think those worship experiences are sealed in my heart and grow sweeter with every remembrance.

Holy, Holy, Holy[54]

> Holy, holy, holy! Lord God Almighty!
> Early in the morning our song shall rise to Thee;
> Holy, holy, holy, merciful and mighty!
> God in three Persons, blessed Trinity!
> Holy, holy, holy! All the saints adore Thee,
> Casting down their golden crowns around the glassy sea;
> Cherubim and seraphim falling down before Thee,
> Who was, and is, and evermore shall be.
> Holy, holy, holy! though the darkness hide Thee,
> Though the eye of sinful man Thy glory may not see;
> Only Thou art holy; there is none beside Thee,
> Perfect in power, in love, and purity.
> Holy, holy, holy! Lord God Almighty!
> All Thy works shall praise Thy Name, in earth, and sky, and sea;
> Holy, holy, holy; merciful and mighty!
> God in three Persons, blessed Trinity!

When talking with someone who is unfamiliar with anything to do with church, the Bible, or the Christian faith, these words might be stumbling blocks, so I think we must understand what we are saying. We might be asked what we mean, and we must be sure to answer honestly. None of us want to make another stumble when we are trying to help them understand what we believe. But sin is sin. Another word really does not fit the bill at all, but we need to understand our sin, so we can give it an understandable name such as lying, cheating, thievery, adultery, lust, and so on. We must guard our words, so the meaning or intensity is real and honest.

---

[54] See Appendix: Music Notes

We should be willing to put ourselves out there to help someone understand what freedom we are talking about and that our message is from the heart.

As an example, a couple words I have worked to understand are atonement and grace. These definitions are a good start at understanding

Atonement is defined as amends made for a wrong, sin, or crime. Reconciliation between parties who are seriously at odds, especially between created beings and a Deity. Or, an instance or cause of such a reconciliation. In a specifically Christian sense, "the Atonement" is the reconciliation between God and humans brought about by the life, death, and resurrection of Jesus of Nazareth, the Christ, the Messiah. The word 'atonement' is used to describe what happens in Exodus 29:36 and Numbers 6:11, in which something is given up to God as repayment for bad actions. To Christians, Jesus is that atoning sacrifice, where Christ is in our place (hence 'substitutionary atonement').[55]

God's grace (and the grace we're called to give) is most aimed at the mud, the scoundrels, and the hurts of daily life. It's not genteel. Grace is undeserved -- you get it when you deserve something less good. That means it is also unjust. Thank God that what goes around doesn't have to come around; otherwise we'd all be sunk.

God's grace is given to all, freely. God gives you the faith that sets you straight, and gives you the Spirit that changes you so you have Christ's goodness. Thus, it is grace that lets loose the riches of God's love.[56]

I never want words to get in the way of the message of Christ. If you need more explanation on any of these terms, or anything else that you hear in church or by a Christian, I encourage you to ask and search for answers. It is a matter of being bold enough to gain the understanding for the meaning of our lives I believe we all seek.

Deny your weakness, and you will never realize God's strength in you.
-Joni Eareckson Tada[57]

55	Spirithome.com
56	Spirithome.com
57	See Appendix: Quote References

7

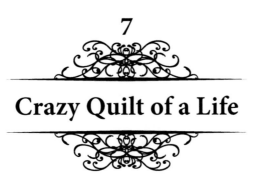

Crazy Quilt of a Life

The beautiful thing about this adventure called faith is that we can count on Him never to lead us astray.
-Charles R. Swindoll

Years ago, I read a portion of the following poem in a book by Corrie ten Boom. More recently, I learned the author is Benjamin Malachi Franklin[58]. When I found some writing by Franklin's grandson, I received permission to add this to my book. The history of this poem, and others written by Franklin, make it more endearing to me. Possibly, because my needlework is usually a mess on the "underside" and I relate. Remember, that is the "fudge" part of my life. I hope this poem inspires you as it has me over many years.

Life is But a Weaving
(Benjamin Malachi Franklin)

>My life is but a weaving
>Between my God and me.
>I cannot choose the colors
>He weaveth steadily.
>Oft' times He weaveth sorrow;
>And I in foolish pride
>Forget He sees the upper
>And I the underside.
>Not 'til the loom is silent
>And the shuttles cease to fly

---

58 See Appendix: Quote References

Will God unroll the canvas
And reveal the reason why.
The dark threads are as needful
In the weaver's skillful hand
As the threads of gold and silver
In the pattern He has planned.

"Getting To Know The Man I Called Papa" is an introduction to the old share crop farmer Benjamin Malachi Franklin who, in 1948, wrote the original words to the poem "The Weaver"

Like most others, I have frequently looked back in time in order to recall my very first childhood memories. Every time I have done so, I always find the man I called "Papa" being ever present, in not only my memories, but in my life as well. He has always been there, and he always will be.

My earliest vision of him is standing in the main street of Kaiser, Arkansas in 1945. He is holding me high above the heads of town's people so I have a better view of them as they burn a straw dummy of a man with a funny mustache.

Papa was at the time, a night watchman in the little town. He lived across the unpaved road from us in an old wooden, shotgun-style house only two houses away from Kaiser's tall city water tank. Although I did not know my daddy much less know he was away at war, I do have vivid memories of Papa being around me at that time.

Although I have vivid memories of Papa during those early years, I cannot recall ever seeing my daddy's face until after he came home from the war. I do remember our family moving from Kaiser to Senath in late 1945 and my daddy driving us to and from Kaiser in order for us to frequently visit Papa and Dora Momma.

While living in Senath we visited him often and continued doing so after both he, and Dora Momma moved from Kaiser into the hill country just outside of Batesville, Arkansas.

By the time I reached the age of eight, Papa had won his argument with my parents regarding my being allowed to stay with him and Dora for a week during the summer of 1948. That first summer stay over would be repeated often during the next seven years of summer school breaks.

In 1950, B. M. Franklin moved from just outside Batesville, Arkansas to the hill country outside Harrisburg, Ark. in order to attend a small cattle farm owned by Raymond Estes, a brother-in-law to one of Papa's sons. Over the next five years I would spend no less than two weeks each summer visiting both he and Dora in their tiny two-room wooden framed house next to a little country cemetery.

Although I do not recall the cemetery's name or exact location, I do recall it being located across a narrow gravel road from a little white church house approximately three miles outside of Harrisburg, Arkansas.

Spending those early summers with him are among my fondest memories. Each visit allowed me to learn and love the real character of this man I called "Papa" and so many people in the surrounding hill country called, "Daddy Ben."

Papa would often hitch his old mule to a small, flat-bottom wooden sled; about the size of an average wooden door, and load me aboard for a three-mile trip into Harrisburg along a winding and hilly, red gravel road.

Frequently, when the desire to see and visit his children and grandchildren overpowered him, he would travel by train or by bus arriving 'unannounced' in the doorway with arms outstretched and a big smile on his face. During such travels, he would often write poems, read his Bible and make notes for discussion. He would later share his poems and notes with his friends at old Brush Arbor church meetings.

I can still see him sitting on his old, wooden front porch late in the day reading to me from his Bible before telling me stories or singing and whistling our favorite old church hymns.

The man I called "Papa" was, in both speech and actions, a man of God as one can easily see in each of his poems.

Although he struggled constantly to survive the hardships of life, I never heard him utter one word of complaint. He simply lived each day of his life without need or care for any material item. To him, life was always spiritual and never carnal.

For a brief, period after 1955, both he and Dora moved to Senath, Missouri. They lived in a small house located across the alley directly behind the drug store that once sat across from the Richmond Theater.

The man I called Papa died on January 1, 1965 after a long struggle with prostate cancer. He (B.M. Franklin) is buried in Bethel Cemetery in his beloved Charleston, Mississippi where he had once raised his young family during the 1920s and 30s.

He often told me, "No one who dies has ever really passed away as long as there is one person remaining on earth who still remembers them."

And, like so many other of his once soft-spoken words, they too would find the way to take deep root inside my very being.

*Bob Corley was born in Osceola, Ark., on Feb. 15, 1940, and left this life on Monday, March 24, 2008, at his residence in Centennial,

Colo. Bob was a member of the Assembly of the Body of Christ.

Bob's family moved to Senath, Mo. when he was only five years old. He spent his young years of growing up in this small town where he had many friends and experiences. He always referred to Senath as his home. This prompted him to write two books about his years spent in Senath as "Reflections in Time."

B. M. Franklin's most popular poem, "The Weaver" has now been put to music by a wonderfully talented gospel singer and songwriter Hazel Kinder. It is available as the lead song on her CD Titled "The Divine Weaver." In Hazel's song, she has written and included several lines of chorus, which are beautifully 'woven' in with the words of the original poem. Franklin's family feels pleased to know the words of his poem have aided in bringing Hazel and many other people peace and comfort during times of pain and sorrow. They only wish he were here to hear her sing the words. The family feels he would be thrilled to know that through Hazel's song and her music the poem is reaching such a large audience.

The commentary addresses the history behind B. M. Franklin's most popular poem "The Weaver"

Commentary by Bob W. Corley November 30, 2006

On B. M. Franklin's most popular poem (Originally Titled) "Just a Weaver"

In 1950, B. M. Franklin (My grandfather) sent his hand-written poem titled "Just A Weaver" to his son in Memphis, Tennessee. He often repeated the same process in order for his poems to be made available to the editor of The Memphis Commercial Appeal Newspaper.

At the time, the newspaper's editor routinely published Franklin's poems in a section of the paper under the column heading titled, "Poet's Corner."

Franklin's son kept that original newspaper paper clipping and Franklin's original hand written poem, together with the envelope (dated 1950) in which Franklin had mailed the poem to him, as cherished family items for almost fifty years.

All three items are now treasured family keepsakes. They are shared in a family keepsake book titled: *The Franklin's Of Tallahatchie County, Mississippi (Circa 1822–2004)*

Jesus Quilt
(Jan Widman)

My quilt has myriad colors and designs; crazy some would say. I prefer to believe these are patterns of my life; acquaintances, dear friends, family, places I've lived and visited, education in all its forms, pets I've loved, and transportation I've used. My varied careers and mundane work have their form here. Life skills, talents, learned behaviors, crafts and techniques each have their own coloration and shape. Different sizes and shapes of fabric are as unique as my fingerprints and the iris in my eyes.

Turning the quilt over, the backing is a plain piece on which all the intricate and beautiful stitches show. Each of those represents prayers offered up for me on any one of thousands of reasons and occasions. They really are seen only on this plain pattern - just as Jesus' love shows best when away from the manic, frantic world pace.

The quilt is bound in one solitary color-peace and unconditional love-representing God's word in my life. Binding up my soul with His word keeps me from coming apart from stress and other outside pressures.

The corners are neatly turned, as if God put His finger down on my life, held me tight and kept me in proper shape (which is actually what He does.)

This piece of put-together fabrics is a distinctive representation of Jesus' influence in my life. Without Him, I am chilled, frazzled, scattered, and not the lovely creation He desires. With His touch in my life, I am confident, loved, secure, and prepared to take on and succeed with whatever He shows me He has for my life.

Grandma's Quilt by
(Louise Thompson)

>Grandmother's quilt was a favorite of mine,
>Covering her old poster bed.
>Pieced together with calico prints
>Of blues and greens and red.
>I still can picture it stretched in the frame
>With the church ladies gathered around,
>Each one so nimbly stitching away
>And never a flaw would be found.
>The quilt frame sat in the big parlor room
>Out of sight behind the closed door,
>Until on a Wednesday the ladies would come
>And take up their quilting once more.
>Each piece was carefully placed on that quilt
>As the finished work came into view.
>And what a joy was in Grandmother's eyes
>When the quilt would make its debut.
>I know there were stitches of love in that quilt

What a beautiful lesson to see.
The pieces each cut with a pattern in mind
And placed there so tenderly.
God's had a plan from the very first day
For the pattern He wants me to be.
Designing my life with parts of Himself
In a style that is special to me.

HINDSIGHT
(Hindsight has its moments.)

Only God Can Touch
(Liz Thompson)

My mind is like an album filled with time and space
When I want to remember, I simply turn the page.
I try to fill the pages, the ones I want to keep,
With lovely thoughts and memories of my life so very sweet.
Sweet, I say, with gladness
I've been given so very much
Gifts of truth and happiness and emotions only God can touch.
January 6, 1997

Writing Serves as Solace Over Decades
(Liz Thompson)
Published in *Suburban News Publications*, **May 6, 2010**

Memories are potent. Experiences with others help form who we become in life.

In March, I spoke to fourth-graders at Grove City Christian School about what it is like to write for a newspaper and to be a writer. They had read "The Landry News" by Andrew Clements. I read it, too, and recommend it for any age. The students were delightful, inquisitive, polite and funny. It was time well spent.

Why did I become a writer? Seems like I was always writing, making up new words to old songs, or imagining the "what ifs." I simply love to write, read, and let my mind run with ideas. Libraries are my friend.

Recently, Dee Weaston Standish, a friend I've known since about 1956 in Westerville, reminded me of the name of the children's book author our Girl Scout troop met; Ellen Snavely, author of "Shoes for Angela." She lived one block from my home on Lincoln Street. I recalled sitting in her living room, listening to her and knowing I wanted to be a writer when I grew up.

I went online to see if I could buy her book and for $50-$75 I sure can. Steven C. Smith lived down the street from me in Westerville and I vaguely remember him as tall, with white hair and a ready smile. He published a 92-page book of poetry, "Life as I See It" and I read it from time-to-time growing up. There is no date of publication in the book but I still enjoy reading his thoughts. After 28 years as a secretary, typing and organizing other people's ideas, I'm taking time to put my own ideas in print. In 1998, I wrote my first column for *Suburban News Publications*. I learned from then Commentary Editor, Cliff Wiltshire how to hone in my thoughts.

Then as a copydesk typist at SNP, I was again typing other people's ideas and was gleefully hooked on reporting – telling other people's stories; my favorite writing. Marty Rozenman, Editor during my stint at SNP, taught me journalism. When I told him I loved reporting, and added I couldn't believe I was getting paid to do something so fun; he said it was amazing people pay us because we know how to put coherent words into sentences and stories. Marty was there during a turning point in my life, cheering me on. He still is.[1]

My one grandmother had a wall of books in her home. My father read constantly and now both parents are avid readers. English teachers in school encouraged me. One does not need to hear to read and since I lost all my hearing by 50, books were always a solace for me; an escape, if you will. My writing became another way of communicating.

These people, and many others, remain in my life. The memories are woven into who I have become. I doubt the Snavely's, Smith's or Thompson's, of this world, write to become famous. I think they have the itch to write and share their thoughts; something to pass on, to make this life better.

God inspires me with a desire to pass on good news. Until those words circling my mind come to a halt, that's what I'll do. My granddaughter, Elizabeth, writes beautifully. The circle remains unbroken.

Marty lost his battle with a rare form of cancer on August 27, 2010. He will be sorely missed but left a legacy on this earth that enriched more lives than I can count with me being one of them.

8

Raise Up Your Voice

*Like newborn babies, crave pure spiritual milk, so that by it
you may grow up in your salvation, now that you have tasted
that the Lord is good.*
-1 Peter 2:2-3

We have talked a lot about listening to God's voice, and now it seems wise to discuss raising our own voice to God. If you are a parent, aunt, uncle, grandparent, step-parent, teacher, or person who has children in your life in any capacity, you know how sweet it is when a child comes to you and asks you a question, tells you a story, asks for your help, draws you a picture, sings you a song, gives you a hug, giggles, smiles, cries, needs a helping hand, or tells you "I love you."

God is our Father, and He wants to hear our stories and our giggles. He wants to hear us tell him we love Him and to ask questions—all the things the children in our lives do with us. Yes, at times we may get angry with Him, but children get angry and frustrated with us, too. Anger's roots often take hold when we don't understand something. Unresolved anger causes a sick feeling in our bodies, and until we work it out with God, we stay sick. We need to keep talking with God, as we might with our parents, spouse, friend, or any loved one. Talking with God is prayer.

When I met my husband in 1977, the only prayers I knew were the "Lord's Prayer," "Now I Lay Me Down to Sleep," and "God is great, God is good, and we thank Him for this food, amen." I knew a myriad of Girl Scout songs we sang at mealtime, but my knowledge of prayers was somewhat lacking.

All my life I talked to God privately, but I didn't really understand that was prayer until Bob told me, "Just talk to God. Thank Him for the food and the day." My voice had been silent in this way for so long, I had much to learn. Bob was patient with me and never laughed.

In 1982, when I made a public confession and became a Christian, Bob and I were baptized together. He was rededicating his life to Christ, and I was a baby in the faith. I was like a dry sponge wanting to soak up knowledge and to understand things I had wondered about my entire thirty years of life.

In Hillcrest Baptist Church in Columbus, Ohio, where we attended, when you sought baptism or wanted to join the church, you attended a class to learn more about your decision. There was one message, during one of those classes, that stuck in my memory. When the pastor was talking to me about sin and I was wondering what my sins really were, at one point, he said, "Garbage in, garbage out." In other words, if we have a daily diet of "garbage," that's what will come out from us—reek from us. Garbage can be defined in many ways, but I see it as filling our minds with negative worldly happenings. If we have a daily diet of God's word and his truths, that is what will come out from us. But it won't reek; it will smell sweet.

But thanks be to God, who always leads us as captives in Christ's triumphal procession and uses us to spread the aroma of the knowledge of him everywhere. For we are to God the pleasing aroma of Christ among those who are being saved and those who are perishing.
-2 Corinthians 2:14-15

Later, when we were joining Gethsemane Lutheran Church, Bob and I attended a "Baptized We Live" membership class. The Lutheran faith and form of worship were completely new to us, and, again, we had a lot to learn. Interestingly, most of the people in the class were apparently longtime Lutherans, and when they learned we were coming from a Baptist church, they had questions for us!

Once, at a women's church meeting, we stood in a circle, and because of my hearing, I only heard part of what we were going to do. Each person would pray, then the next, and on around the circle. My hearing loss was such that I only heard pieces of conversations. Any confidence I had was waning, and I knew I would mess it up. When it seemed to be my turn, I prayed something, but my eyelids were fluttering wildly. This continued each time I was asked to pray aloud. I was terrified.

In time, I learned to let others know about my hearing loss and my feelings about being asked to pray aloud. Then several women explained the process and the fact that I didn't need to pray if I was uncomfortable. When the pressure was off and I understood my fear, the fear dissipated. In time, I was able to pray when it was my turn. I realized God understood my fear, and when I read that the Spirit groans for us whenever we don't know how to pray, I was comforted.

> *In the same way, the Spirit helps us in our weakness. We do not know what we ought to pray for, but the Spirit himself intercedes for us through wordless groanings.*
> *Romans 8:26*

God is gracious and gives us gifts. When we use those gifts to honor God, we please Him; the same way a parent is glad when a child uses a gift for good.

I remember reading the following in a church bulletin years ago. I saved it for years, shedding tears every time I found it again. In the following excerpt, Stefenie Jacks uses Erma Bombeck's "Children are like Kites" to share her story in hopes of spreading the word about the condition her son lives with.

> I see children as kites. You spend a lifetime trying to get them off the ground. You run with them until you're both breathless...they crash...they hit the rooftop...you patch and comfort, adjust and teach.
>
> You watch them lifted by the wind and assure them that someday they'll fly. Finally, they are airborne: they need more string and you keep letting it out. But with each twist of the ball of twine, there is a sadness that goes with joy. The kite becomes more distant, and you know it won't be long before that beautiful creature will snap the lifeline that binds you together and will soar as it is meant to soar, free and alone.
>
> Only then do you know that you did your job.

> Logan was diagnosed at two weeks old with Complex Congenital Heart Defects. We were shocked to learn he had five very complex defects: D-Transposition of the Great Arteries, Double Outlet Right Ventricle, VSD, Pulmonary Stenosis, and a Right Aortic Arch.
>
> He underwent three open heart surgeries, the BT Shunt (4 weeks old), Rastelli Procedure with RV-PA reconstruction using a Contegra Conduit (10 months old), and RVOT muscle bundle resection with RV-PA conduit with a 19mm pulmonary

homograft (3 yrs old).

Logan has also undergone multiple caths and a balloon angioplasty, had a Mickey Button feeding tube for eighteen months, and also suffered numerous complications from his previous surgeries that included focal seizures, bloody stools, pericardial effusion, and Dressler's Syndrome. He has since recovered from all of his post surgical complications.

Logan also currently sees a speech therapist to help with a speech delay.

We face an uphill battle with Logan, but no matter how high the mountains are that we face, we have hope! He is a brave little boy and our hero!

Before Logan came along, I never knew that the world of CHD existed, nor did I know how very common heart defects are, affecting one out of every one hundred births.

My life has changed so much since his birth, going from full-time career mom to full time stay-at-home mom/chauffeur to a special needs child. While this is not the path in life that I had originally chosen, I feel so blessed that it chose me.

This crazy roller coaster ride we know as Congenital Heart Defects has taken us on some crazy twists and turns along the way, but it has ultimately led us on the most amazing journey. We have met so many brave and wonderful families just like us, and because of them, we have hope.

I created this blog after using my son's care page for a few years but wanted to expand to reach more families out there. With 40,000 babies being born each year to CHD, there will be many finding themselves braving these rough waters looking for someone to throw them a life raft. The goal is to provide hope to those finding themselves on this journey and remind them that they too can find joy.[59]

As we go through our lives, growing and learning, we need someone to hold our kite string. Once we reach an understanding of God, we realize he has been there all along, in all circumstances. So often we feel like we are floating around, lost, purposeless, when God is always there watching and waiting for us to hand him the string.

---

59 Whenlifehandsyouabrokenheart.blogspot.com

9

God's Word for Us

God did not write a book and send it by messenger to be read at a distance by unaided minds. He spoke a Book and lives in His spoken words, constantly speaking His words and causing the power of them to persist across the years.
A. W. Tozer[60]

We need the Spirit of God in us. He wants us to read Scripture where He talks to us. As it says in 2 Timothy 3:16-17, "All scripture is God-breathed and is useful for teaching, rebuking, correcting and training in righteousness, so that the servant of God may be thoroughly equipped for every good work." Just as God breathed life into the Scripture, we need to breathe in the words God gave us. This Scripture reminds me of a hymn my daughter and I used to sing together, harmonizing.

Breathe on me Breath of God[61]
(Lyrics by Edwin Hatch and music by Robert Jackson, 1878)

>Breathe on me, breath of God,
>Fill me with life anew,
>That I may love what Thou dost love,
>And do what Thou wouldst do.
>Breathe on me, breath of God,
>Until my heart is pure,
>Until with Thee I will one will,

---

60 See Appendix: Quote References
61 See Appendix: Music Notes

To do and to endure.
Breathe on me, breath of God,
Blend all my soul with Thine,
Until this earthly part of me
Glows with Thy fire divine.
Breathe on me, breath of God,
So shall I never die,
But live with Thee the perfect life
Of Thine eternity.

    I look at life as a journey. We all begin as children, and as we age, we learn differently and, with God's help, mature in our faith. In school, we ask questions of our teachers to understand the subjects we are taught: math, science, reading, writing, history, art, music, and more. I remember doubting that I would ever use what they were teaching. Much of schooling seemed mundane and useless, at the time of learning. When I began learning American Sign Language, the first lesson was numbers. I literally thought this was a waste of time since we don't talk in numbers, so I didn't practice very much. The next week, the teacher asked us to share our phone numbers, addresses, ages, number of children or grandchildren and times of the day. I learned quickly and with embarrassment.

    Our doubts and questions sometimes make us lazy or apathetic. Months or years later, or even days later as shown above, reality can smack us in the face when we realize how much we need to learn. It feels good, too, when a quote from a poet seems familiar and relevant in our lives, when we solve a problem at our work place and cannot quite recall where we gained that skill. Maybe your child or grandchild asks you a question you can answer because you studied your math, history, literature, grammar, or spelling in school. If you don't have the answers, likely you know where and how to find them, or during your lifetime of education, you learned how to reason. That's the process of learning and growing.

    So it is with studying Scripture. No matter when our learning begins, we have a starting point. When was yours? If it was yesterday, then you are at the start of your trek. If your journey began years ago, think about what you have learned and how you are applying Scripture to your life. If you have put Scripture learning aside because life got too busy, pick up that Bible today and read. That's what I did, and then I wanted to learn more. I use a concordance, which is an index of topics in the Bible, and follow themes throughout the Bible. I might take the word "forgiveness" and start in the Old Testament following it through the New Testament.

It calls for self-motivation, but it is possible. I always gravitated toward Bible studies and classes at whatever church we belonged to. Little by little, I began to love to pick up the Bible and read it. When I read Scripture, or hear it read, I find it soothing and fulfilling. I am often challenged by the words I read or hear. I don't want to ever get so comfortable in my faith that I think I have nothing to learn. I love it when I read or hear verses from the Bible and find myself nodding in agreement or having a wake-up call on my behavior. It means I'm alive and growing.

One night, as I was going to sleep, I realized I could not remember ever reading the first Psalm. The next morning, I read it and continued to read more and more of the Psalms. I purchased a good study Bible, and on the same page as the Scripture, there are explanations for each verse. This has helped me immensely. For example, here is John 3:16 and the study Bible's notations below it.

John 3:16: "For God so loved the world that he gave his one and only Son, that whoever believes in him shall not perish but have eternal life."

Study notes: God so loved the world. The great truth that motivated God's plan of salvation. (compare to 1 John 4:9-10). world. All people on earth--or perhaps all creation (see notes on 1:4,9). gave his one and only Son. Compare Isaiah 9:6 ("a son is given," referring to the Messianic Son of David--who is also God's Son (see 25a 7:14 and note). See also 1:14, 18 and notes; compare Genesis 22:2, 16; Romans 8:32 and notes. Although believers are also called "sons" of God (2 Corinthians 6:18; Galatians 4:5-6), Jesus is God's Son in a unique sense (see 20:31 and note).[62]

As you can see, you can delve deeply into every verse of the Bible, using the study Bible to compare verses to others for clarification.

My journey continues as I hope yours will.

Today, if you hear his voice, do not harden your hearts.
-Hebrews 4:7

---

[62] Zondervan NIV Study Bible, 2008 Update, Grand Rapids, Michigan, General Editor, Kenneth L. Barker, Page 2188, Large Print Version

SILENCE

God speaks in the silence of the heart. Listening is the beginning of prayer.
-Mother Teresa[63]

When reading this quote by Mother Teresa, I am reminded once again of the years of literal silence in my life. Losing my hearing gradually since childhood allowed me time to develop communication skills, such as reading lips, body language, and, later in life, American Sign Language. In the hearing world, only a selective few use sign language—interpreters for the Deaf and family of a deaf person. Curiosity draws some people to learn sign language, but like any other language, if you don't use it, you lose it. Many of the hard of hearing people I have met refused to learn sign language because, as I have been told numerous times, "I'm not deaf!" I've always been a self-starter without needing approval from others to learn something or to challenge myself. When I developed a certain fear of silence, learning sign language sent that fear into the shadows. Even though I lived in the hearing world, knowing this language gave me a new form of expression. I was quick to teach basics to my hearing counterparts at work and in my personal life.

When I was in my late forties, I was sure that worship would elude me. My husband was retelling sermons to me after services, and I was no longer in choir since I could not hear myself. This was a lonely time for me, but I felt God's presence in my life. He showed me blessings every day even though I was living and working in the hearing world. The beauty of nature was more profound, and God gave me many poems to write that comforted me, as well as praising Him.

She's Thankful to be Hearing the World that Eluded Her[64] (Liz Thompson)

About fifteen years ago, when my husband and I walked through the door of Gethsemane Lutheran Church, we knew that the move was right for us. We had Baptist and Methodist backgrounds, so the switch was notable in our faith journey. I, of course, joined the choir, in part because Ron Kenreich

---

63 See Appendix: Quote References
64 Published in *The Columbus Dispatch*, November 22, 2008.

was the organist.

Ron directed the choir during my last year at Westerville High School (now Westerville South). When we met again at Gethsemane more than twenty years later, he still remembered me as Liz Day from his first year of teaching at our school.

By 1996, though, I knew I had to quit the church choir. I could no longer hear myself or the singer next to me. My inability to understand spoken words had begun during childhood, and I was wearing two hearing aids.

Bob, my husband, and I were glad to be sitting together at last during the services. We'd kneel when prayers were spoken by a pastor, who would say after a few lines, "Lord, in your mercy." We'd reply in unison, "Hear our prayer." In time, my husband realized that I wasn't saying the response, even though my head was lowered in prayer. I couldn't understand anything being said, so I was saying my own prayers.

Sensing my needs, on Sunday after the pastor spoke his words, Bob pressed my hand gently. I looked at him, and he smiled. I saw that touch as love and adoration spoken from God through Bob. Tears spilled down my cheeks.

From then on, when he pressed my hand, I spoke the response. Bob started giving me a synopsis of the sermon, filling in the blanks of what I'd missed in the message. Eventually, though, we knew that another change was needed.

The solution eluded us until, while driving on Morse Road one day, I saw a sign for Holy Cross Lutheran Church of the Deaf. I summoned enough courage to drive into the parking lot on that sunny Saturday, then marched to the door with purpose, and knocked. I knocked again. I peeked through the window and saw people inside.

Why weren't they answering? As quickly as I wondered, the idea hit me: "They're deaf, Liz." Just then, someone saw me and came to the door.

Bob and I worshipped there for the next year, learning and growing in our faith. My signing improved, too. Still, although words were spoken and signed at Holy Cross and my husband wasn't the only hearing person in the congregation, he missed worshipping in a hearing church.

One Sunday, we returned to Gethsemane. Seeing old friends felt good, but I understood nothing. By then, I was truly deaf, even with my hearing aids.

We faced the challenge together, deciding that our worship had to be at home until we could find another solution.

We knew that God understood.

In 2002, I became a candidate for a cochlear implant. My only question: "How soon can I have the surgery?" The operation proved successful. In a quiet setting, I could understand nearly ninety-five percent of a conversation—a vast improvement from zero percent in the implanted ear and eight percent in the other.

I keep a healthy supply of batteries on hand for the voice processor. When the batteries die, I am still deaf.

With every bird song, every child's voice, or any other sound I missed for years, I am reminded of this blessing. And I won't forget the kindnesses that others showed when I couldn't hear anything: a smile, an explanation in writing, or a sign of love and caring in a simple touch. Thanks for listening for me.

Since these experiences noted above, I have received another implant in my other ear. My ability to hear and understand has increased even more. Such a blessing. Music was a strong part of my life until my eventual deafness. Once I had the implants, I felt sure music would return, but I soon learned that music sounded flat and hearing different pitches was elusive for me. I struggled with this fact until recently when Cochlear Americas offered a DVD and CD written by Richard Reed called *Hope Notes*[65]. Richard was a musician prior to his deafness, and he also received a cochlear implant. He developed these products to help people like me learn to hear music again! I found myself laughing with joy while watching the DVD giving me a visual of note progression and familiar songs. His gift and love of music nudged him to help others relearn music with implants. Thank God my music memory is strong, and songs run through my head often. When I voice these songs, the tonality is usually off key, but I won't give up. Richard's gift to those of us with CIs is one that will help many people regain a new appreciation for listening and performing music.

Still Music
(Liz Thompson)

> Still music—
> Silence without and singing within,
> Laughter not heard but only seen.

---

[65] See Appendix: Suggested Reading and Websites

Never a stanza—
Not one word,
Like the distant trilling of a lone, red bird.
Humming creates sensations of rhyme,
Hopes of bright music with meter and time.
Vibrations chill through me,
A feeling divine,
Realizing the silence will not last
Through all time.
Silence—not frightening
But a blessed relief,
And memories fill spaces that to others seem bleak.
Music, sweet music,
Can be felt and not seen
When one reaches within
To what is pure and clean.

SILENT FORGIVENESS

For many years, I had harbored anger toward some people in my life. These people abused their power over me, and I was carrying a heart full of hurt, anger, and confusion because of it. The details are not necessary to the story. Just know, I felt that there was nothing that could be done with my feelings, and they were justified, even to God. I had convinced myself I would have to live with this the rest of my life. A pastor had advised me that, if these people did not ask me for forgiveness, I could never forgive them. God showed me a different response, and I listened.

One day during services at Holy Cross Lutheran Church for the Deaf, we were saying and signing the Lord's Prayer. When we got to the part, "...forgive us our debts, as we also have forgiven our debters," my arms dropped to my sides. I stood there, mute and still, staring at the cross at the front of this small church. I finally understood what those words meant. If I could not forgive others, how could God forgive me? It was me who changed, not the other people. My heart was softened, and forgiveness filled the place where hurt had been. This action didn't change or remove the memories, but my life was freed of those chains of hate and unforgiveness. Thank God! There is no other way I could have experienced this sense of forgiveness and freedom. It was nothing I did. It was God's doing, and my heart filled with His love.

Churches use different versions, but, whether it is "forgive us our sins," "forgive us our trespasses," or "forgive us our debts," it has the same meaning.

The Lord's Prayer

We were new in 2010 to Beautiful Savior Lutheran Church in Grove City, Ohio. Each church we have been blessed to be a part of has taught us something new about ourselves and about worshipping God. This is part of the personal journey. The following was printed in the bulletin for us to follow and to read aloud in unison. This helped me understand more about the way God wants us to pray and how this prayer is tucked in my heart and mind to stay.

Our Father in heaven...
With these words, God tenderly invites us to believe that He is our true Father and that we are His true children, so that we may pray to Him as boldly and confidently as dear children ask their dear father.

hallowed be your name...
God's name is kept holy when His Word is taught in its truth and purity, and we, as children of God, lead holy lives according to it. Help us to do this dear Father in heaven! But whoever teaches and lives contrary to God's Word dishonors God's name among us. Keep us from doing this, dear Father in heaven!

your kingdom come...
God's kingdom comes when our heavenly Father gives His Holy Spirit, so that, by His grace, we believe His holy Word and lead a godly life now on earth and forever in heaven.

your will be done, on earth as it is in heaven...
God's will is done when He breaks and defeats every evil plan and purpose of the devil, the world, and our sinful flesh, which try to prevent us from keeping God's name holy and letting His kingdom come. And God's will is done when He strengthens and keeps us firm in His Word and in the faith as long as we live. This is His good and gracious will.

Give us today our daily bread...
God surely gives daily bread without our asking, even to all the wicked, but we pray in this petition that He would lead us to realize this and to receive our daily bread with thanksgiving.

And forgive us our debts, as we also have forgiven our debtors...
We pray in this petition that our Father in heaven would not look upon our sins or because of them deny our prayers, for we are worthy of none of the things for which we ask, neither have we deserved them, but we ask that He would give them all to use by grace. For we daily sin much and surely deserve nothing but

punishment. So we too will forgive from the heart and gladly do good to those who sin against us.

And lead us not into temptation...

God surely tempts no one to sin, but we pray in this petition that God would guard and keep us, so that the devil, the world, and our flesh may not deceive us or lead us into false belief, despair, and other great and shameful sins; and though we are tempted by them, we pray that we may overcome and win the victory.

but deliver us from the evil one...

In conclusion, we pray in this petition that our Father in heaven would deliver us from every evil that threatens body and soul, property and reputation, and finally when our last hour comes, grant us a blessed end and graciously take us from this world of sorrow to Himself in heaven.

We can be sure that these petitions are acceptable to our Father in heaven and are heard by Him, for He Himself has commanded us to pray in this way and has promised to hear us. Therefore we say, "Amen. Yes, it shall be so."

WOW

We do wrap ourselves up in the world; after all, the world is where we physically exist. It is what we know and see every day.

Buckeye Christian Church's WOW (Women of the Word) Sunday school class was studying the book *Heaven* by Randy Alcorn. Our teacher, Christy Kirtlan, was talking about different ways of worshiping. We discussed singing traditional music of familiar hymns versus praise worship with a praise band and singers.

"Those who listen to the old hymns aren't more holy than those who clap their hands, stand, or raise their hands in the air," she said. "We are all worshiping God. When I raise my hands in the air when I'm praying or singing, it reminds me of when my girls were little and would come to me with their arms up and say, "Uppy, Mommy, uppy!" and I'd pick them up and hold them. God is my Father, and when I raise my arms, I'm like my girls were, wanting God to hold me.

This struck me as a remarkable and visual expression of her faith and a reminder that we need to take care not to judge how others worship.

Another comment made by a different woman in our class caused me to chuckle, "When we get to heaven, God's not going to say 'OK, those of you who want to hear traditional music, over here, and those of you who want to hear praise music over here.'" God knows our hearts, and if they are focused on Him, He is listening.

Alcorn's book *Heaven* answered many questions for me. I always was confused about our heavenly and earthly bodies. How can a dead person whose body has decomposed be brought to life? Will we go directly to heaven and see Jesus? Is that where my loved ones who have died are today? I really can't answer all those questions, but I know with God all things are possible and that His plans are greater than anything I could possibly imagine.

The Bible tells us that when Jesus was on the cross, He told one thief on the cross near Him that that day He would be in paradise with Him. Alcorn confirms that when he writes that, when we die, our spirit either goes into God's presence or is separated from Him. Unless Christ comes again before we die, we will go to what theologians call the present heaven. Alcorn referred to Ecclesiastes 12:7, "The dust returns to the ground it came from, and the spirit returns to God who gave it" and Philippians 1:23, "I am torn between the two: I desire to depart and be with Christ, which is better by far" where Paul referred to dying and being with Christ. Alcorn also references 2 Corinthians 5:8, "... would prefer to be away from the body and at home with the Lord."

Alcorn's teachings are all Biblically supported, and I began to learn that, when I die, I will be with Christ. My body will be in a wait mode. The description of heaven tells us that our bodies won't have the same needs as they do when we were living on Earth. Reading the description of heaven in Revelations tells us it will be beautiful. Alcorn's books, fiction and non-fiction, describe for us Biblically what heaven will be like. But I believe we are only given a glimpse of what it will be like. I'm not sure we humans could comprehend the enormity of it. The hymn, "When We See Christ" comes to mind.

> It will be worth it all when we see Jesus,
> Life's trials will seem so small when we see Christ;
> One glimpse of His dear face all sorrow will erase,
> So bravely run the race till we see Christ. [66]

Christy led the WOW class through the book using the Bible just as Randy Alcorn uses Scripture throughout his book. Her teaching, the questions and comments from our class members, and the reading book, led me to my greater understanding of heaven. It was freeing for me, and my eyes were opened in such

---

66   See Appendix: Music Notes

a way that talking about death no longer troubles me. Certainly, the death of a loved one is a great loss for us who are left behind, but if these people died knowing Jesus as their Savior, we know they will be waiting for us. This provides comfort for me if I know these people had given his or her life over to God.

We must be cautious how we tell others about our faith. The best advice is to tell our story, how we learned about Jesus, and what believing in Him as the Son of God means in our life.

Christy challenged our class at the beginning of the *Heaven* study to raise our hand if we knew how to answer the questions of others about Jesus. Only a few hands shot up at first and more at the end of the study.

Christy wrote, later, "The Bible tells us that the Lord is not slow in keeping his promise, but that he is patient with us, not wanting anyone to perish (in Hell), but everyone to come to repentance (2 Peter 3:9 "The Lord is not slow in keeping his promise, as some understand slowness. He is patient with you, not wanting anyone to perish, but everyone to come to repentance")."[67] I believe God is waiting for all to hear of His saving grace, and we are all called to tell our story of how we were saved and have the hope of heaven. When all have heard and have the opportunity to name Jesus Christ as their Savior, then we will be restored to life for eternity with God. Everyone must hear, and everyone must make a choice.

But in your hearts revere Christ as Lord. Always be prepared to give an answer to everyone who asks you to give the reason for the hope that you have. But do this with gentleness and respect.
-1 Peter 3:15

Tell Your Story

I have heard people of faith talk about "witnessing," and I wondered if I could actually do that if a situation presented itself to me. One definition is telling the truth about something you have seen, like witnessing a car accident and giving a report to the police. Since I know the truth of what I believe, the words should come easily, it seems. But I have learned that God does surprise us and place us where He wants us to be for His purposes, not ours.

In the last few years, I have gone outside my comfort zone and told people about my faith, hopefully in a way they understood. Be-

---

[67] Christy's message was an email

fore I speak a word, I send a silent prayer asking God for the words this person needs to hear. Each time God has placed me somewhere, the words seem to come naturally. In retrospect, I can always see how God put the words in my mind and mouth. My lead-ins to conversations with people seeking the truth vary with each circumstance. I might ask if a person ever prays, if they belong to a church, or if they like to read, leading into reading the Bible. When face-to-face, I can tell if the questions hit the mark, so we have a friendly confrontation.

At a conference, Heather, a beautiful, blond-haired young woman was telling me how frustrated she was that she didn't have a boyfriend or even the prospect of one. She and I had one thing in common—we both struggle with multiple sclerosis, a chronic central nervous system disease. When she stopped talking and seemed to say she was out of options, then I spoke.

"Do you pray?" I said.

"Oh, I know I should. I haven't gone to church," she replied somewhat defensively and apologetically. She avoided eye contact and seemed to hunch over a bit.

"Going to church is not what I asked. Do you have a personal relationship with God?" I added.

"Not really. Not like I should. I have been looking into Eastern religions and Buddhism. I find it fascinating."

My antenna went up. Weeks prior to this conversation, our pastor had completed a series on world religions and how people are searching for the "right fit." I knew right then that God had put me in that conversation for a reason. He had prepared me.

"It's good to search, but I hope your search stops with God and His Son Jesus."

She was crying now and was very distraught. I remained calm, a real mother figure because she was the same age as my daughter. I know some of her personal history—that she has had live-in boyfriends, been a real partier, traveled Europe through unconventional ways, and more. Standing before me, I saw a beautiful, bright woman who was quite lost. I prayed for the words, and I told her what I knew.

"Do you know that God loves you?" I said. She kept crying. "He does love you, and He sent His only son to die for you. He loves you that much." I paused and waited. She was silent.

"I hope you know that you are God's child, and He created you for a purpose on this earth. He will listen to you anytime you talk to Him. About anything, even finding a decent boyfriend," I added smiling.

She finally spoke. "Are you sure He loves me?" I nodded yes. She cried some more.

"He is right here with you, and all you need to do is talk with Him."

Soon she let me know that the conversation was over. We were at a party-like gathering, and I'm quite sure she never expected to have this conversation with me. I hugged her, and she moved on.

I felt sure she was ignoring me after that, but I knew I had followed God's urging because I know He placed me right in front of her.

The next day, I saw her in the elevator, and she didn't look too well. I asked how she was, and she told me she had stayed up too late the night before partying. I suggested she get some rest, and in that way, I showed concern and love for her.

I prayed there would be another opportunity for us to talk, and when there was not, I hoped someone else would be there for her when she returned home.

Another time, I was at a book signing along with other local authors. We had very few people attend, so we sipped coffee and chatted while we waited. I caught two of the women talking about the Book of Revelations, the last book in the Bible. The scenario went something like this:

"Oh, I could never read Revelations! The end of the world is so frightening to think about," Tess said to the other woman.

"I agree. All that fire and horses and stuff, it's terrifying to think about!" Sydney replied.

I waited to see where the conversation was headed. The discussion kept up like this, and I finally interjected. "You haven't read Revelations then?"

"No way!" they both replied, surprised I asked.

Here is another time God had prepared me for this moment. Our WOW Sunday school class was nearing the end of our study of the book *Heaven* by Randy Alcorn. What flowed from my mouth next truly was God speaking through me because my thoughts were so clear and I didn't need to stop and think before I spoke.

"Have either of you read the book *Heaven* by Randy Alcorn?" I asked.

"No, is it good?" Remember, these were both authors.

"Our Sunday school class, Women of the Word, is studying it, and so many of my questions about heaven and the end times are being answered. I recommend it," I said.

Sydney slowly moved and changed seats, starting another conversation just out of earshot of us.

I turned to Tess and looked at her face for a clue if she wanted me to continue. She seemed to be searching so I continued.

"Are you really fearful of the end times?" I asked gently.

"Yes, I am. I don't even like to talk about it much," Tess said, still with interest in her voice.

"Well, I recommend the book or maybe the Left Behind series, even though it is fiction. (Note that the authors of the Left Behind series took liberties in their writing that does not completely follow the Bible. Please keep this in mind when reading these books.) Something that will give you a clear idea of what the Bible says," I said and paused. "But what I have learned is that we need not fear death or the end times if we have asked Jesus to come into our heart."

She sat looking at me. I continued more fervently now.

"Do you and your husband have a church you call home?" I asked. This was just an opening for me to see what she understood.

"Not right now. We are kind of looking but haven't found one we like yet," Tess said cautiously.

I invited her to our church and asked if she knew where it was located. She did.

"I know God doesn't want you to be scared. I hate to see you so frightened when all you have to do is ask Jesus to come into your heart to stay. Tell Him you know you have done things wrong and want to change, learn, and grow." I went on to tell her that I made that decision when I was thirty even though I was raised in a home where we went to church.

My words flowed, like I said, and I could feel it was the right thing to do and say, but it appeared to be missing the mark. I backed off a bit and told her that I truly believed everything I had said and hoped it made sense to her and that if she ever wanted to talk, I'd listen. If she ever wanted to visit our church, she would be welcomed warmly.

It was not about me, it was about Tess and all the other Tess's in the world.

Music, Music, Music

One of the first songs God inspired me to write, "Stepping Stones," explains my feelings about telling others about our faith.

Stepping Stones[68]

I asked the Lord to use me to witness and proclaim His love and tender mercies and His wondrous plan.

Chorus 1: I may be a stepping-stone for someone seeking You. Dear Lord, I pray when they hear me, they'll feel Your love come through.

---

[68] Based on a poem with the same name "Stepping Stones"

"Be ready," was His answer, and I turned around to see
Someone seeking for the Lord, and they wondered how they could be free.
I heard their pain, their loneliness, their searching soul astray.
I quickly prayed to God for words that He would have me say.

Chorus 2: I may be a stepping-stone for someone seeking You.
Dear Lord, I pray the words I speak will only be from You.
I told them of my faith and how my life had changed so much
since I'd heard God call my name and in the Lord I put my trust.

Chorus 3: I may be a stepping-stone for someone seeing You.
Dear Lord, I pray when they see me they're really seeing You.
Jesus showed us what to do, we only have to pray,
Please use me Lord this very day, and He'll show you the way.
So when a stranger comes your way and you know not where they've been,
Give them your smile and loving care, God's love makes you their friend.

Final Chorus: We may be a stepping-stone for someone seeking You. Dear Lord we pray when they meet us, they'll turn their hearts to You. We may be a stepping-stone for someone seeking You. Dear Lord, we pray, when they meet us, they'll feel like meeting You.

My Salvation Story
(Jan Widman[69])

I got Jesus in my life because people prayed for me.
There were times I really wanted to ask—but I was afraid.
Fearful of the unknown, wary of what would be said, I kept my desire hid
Till one day I bowed my head.
I knew there was something missing;
I'd known for quite some time.
But how do you reveal that need when you want to appear "just fine"?
Really now, what would people think if I shared my need to fill that vacuum?
Well, I wasn't that brave—not yet.

---

[69]   See Appendix: Contributor Biographies

Finally, on a warm June day, the preacher spoke of Hell.
He said that's where I'd spend my days—after death I mean—
If I didn't take time to tell God I was sorry for all the sins I'd done.
I needed to ask forgiveness, ask Jesus His only begotten Son
To come into my life and be my Lord and King.
This time there was no doubt for me;
I got down on my knees.
I asked Jesus into my heart that day, and to forgive my sins—can you please?
When I rose again and turned, I knew the work was done.
I felt the vacuum place full now—the work of God and His Son.
God even told me of my life's career as I left the church that day.
I was amazed, surprised, and pleased.
Wouldn't have wanted any other way!
The road to the new career was hard—bumpy and full of holes.
God provided the ways and means.
I sort of let Him be in control.
All those years would take too many words, so I'll tell you how it's gone.
There were days when I yielded to Him
And days when I did not.
Decisions got made that had His mark
And many more were blots of tears and stains of stress and fear, yet when I see it now,
I can tell you without a qualm that asking Jesus into my life
was the best, the very best, decision I have ever made.
There are no regrets about it.
And I've learned He loves me unconditionally, doesn't reject me, loves me when I'm "a pill,"
and I love Him so terribly much, and I know I always will.
That day was June's first Sunday in 1971, Tallmadge, OH, Methodist Church. Preaching was Rev. P. C. Clark, who had had a stroke previously making his words unclear, but they certainly were to my heart and soul.

BEING A CHRISTIAN IS NOT BORING...

It is for freedom that Christ has set us free. Stand firm, then, and do not let yourselves be burdened again by a yoke of slavery.
-Galatians 5:1

Some non-Christians believe that living a Christian life is restricting, simply not fun, and definitely boring. That is far from the truth.

Living as Christ wants us to live has a pure freedom that is difficult to put into words. That is one reason that living a Christ-like life is a wonderful way to show others it's a fulfilling way to live. We make mistakes, we sin, we stumble and fall because we are human. Hopefully, we learn from these mistakes and don't repeat them. If our eyes are open to the real Truth, when we sin, it will be evident to us quickly.

More than once, I have heard that the true character of a person is revealed during a crisis. This makes sense to me because, if our minds and hearts are filled with anger and bitterness, when we meet an obstacle, that bitterness can spill out. When we get a flat tire, fall and injure ourselves, are fired, or reprimanded at our workplace, or any number of situations, chances are we will react with anger, yelling, cursing, slamming things, accusing others, and stomping about. I have done that, haven't you? Be honest with yourself, and admit it. I had a temper and was quick to yell, slam doors, and stop listening to anything but my frustration.

I'm not saying that I'm perfect "now," just that I was more imperfect in my past. My anger today is generally when I see man's inhumanity to man or blatant cruelty in our lives. I learned to control my temper and my tongue. It was not easy, and it took a long time. I still slip but quickly realize my sin, stop, ask for forgiveness, and do what I can to make amends. I must choose to control my thoughts.

We demolish arguments and every pretension that sets itself up against the knowledge of God, and we take captive every thought to make it obedient to Christ.
-2 Corinthians 10:5

Like those caterpillars in the corner of Andrew's jar, all bound in white cocoons and huddled together, it's easy for humans to huddle with others who are bound up, frustrated, and angry. We feed off each other's anger, and ours grows.

In the last few years, I have broken an arm, dislocated a shoulder, and broken both my wrists. These were accidents most likely occurring because I live with multiple sclerosis and my balance just "ain't what it used to be." In 2009, a friend of ours was painting our bedroom. I was in the kitchen a couple rooms away when I fell backwards onto hardwood flooring. I spread my left hand back to "break" the fall, since I had broken my right wrist two years prior.

The pain made me cry out, and when I looked at my wrist, it was twisted and swollen. Believe me, it hurt. Our friend, Tom, came running. I had fallen into the dog's water dish and was lying in water but didn't really mind. There I was splayed on the floor, lying in water, my dog licking my face, and Tom asking me what he could do.

"Let me just lay here, and if you will, call Bob," I said.

Watching my pain, Tom was more upset than me. But he called Bob, who was on his way home.

"What can I do, Liz?" Tom said. I showed him my wrist and told him I needed to rest, catch my breath, and, when Bob got home, I'd get up. Tom helped me rise to a sitting position and talked with me. At that point, I had one cochlear implant external device in my hand when I fell—I was deaf and reading his lips. I asked him to replace the batteries for me, and I talked him through the process.

Now Tom is a tall man, and his hands were shaking, making the task difficult. He accomplished the battery change, and I placed it on my ear. He got a towel to soak up the water, and we waited.

I hope you chuckle when you read what I asked Tom after all that.

"Tom, what did I say when I fell? Did I curse or anything?"

"No, Liz, you moaned and didn't say a thing," Tom said. Tom is a Christian, and I didn't have to explain why I asked this. That was comforting. I often wondered if, caught off guard or in a situation like this, I would defer to old language. I have worked at shoving all that away and replacing it with good things. Not that my tongue was hasty to curse, but I did use a few choice words on occasion. I was so pleased my tongue didn't spew anything I would regret.

When I say, "I am a Christian"[70]

> When I say, "I am a Christian,"
> I'm not shouting, "I've been saved!"
> I'm whispering, "I get lost!
> That's why I chose this way."
> When I say, "I am a Christian,"
> I don't speak with human pride.
> I'm confessing that I stumble—
> Needing God to be my guide.
> When I say, "I am a Christian,"
> I'm not trying to be strong.
> I'm professing that I'm weak
> And pray for strength to carry on.
> When I say, "I am a Christian,"
> I'm not bragging of success.

---

[70] Used by Permission, Copyright 1988 Carol Wimmer.

I'm admitting that I've failed
And cannot ever pay the debt.
When I say, "I am a Christian,"
I don't think I know it all.
I submit to my confusion
Asking humbly to be taught.
When I say, "I am a Christian,"
I'm not claiming to be perfect.
My flaws are all too visible
But God believes I'm worth it.
When I say, "I am a Christian,"
I still feel the sting of pain.
I have my share of heartache,
Which is why I seek His name.
When I say, "I am a Christian,"
I do not wish to judge.
I have no authority...
I only know I'm loved.

We can read Scripture every day and hold it in our hearts, but sometimes it jumps at us and we think, "Why didn't I see that before?" This following story by my daughter, Mary, brought tears to my eyes. I have known of her struggles and felt partly to blame. My temper was once out of control. I could "blow up" for no real reason and feel regret afterwards, wondering how in the world I could stop it. When I was thirty, I became a Christian, and the Bible began to open my eyes that nothing in "this world" could help me. Only God could.

Temper my Temper
(Mary Dunkel[71])

I never considered myself to be an angry person. In fact, I actually considered myself to be quite humble, with a gentle, quiet spirit. But, there I sat one morning, kneeling at the foot of my bed crying out to the Lord to calm my temper that I had once again allowed to rage at my three young children. I absolutely adored those sweet little ones; they were my treasure, my greatest joy in life. I enjoyed their company so much that, rather than bustle them off to preschool and kindergarten, I had kept them home to teach them. We spent our days taking

---

71   See Appendix: Contributor Biographies

nature walks, reading wonderful books, singing songs, and playing games. Yet, somehow the gentle, quiet spirit that I always thought I had seemed to vanish when one of these little blessings crossed my plans for the day.

They were ages five, four, and two when this battle with my anger overwhelmed me. As a new believer, I was face to face with how ugly my sins were, and I didn't like what I saw. I was deeply troubled by the realization that, no matter how hard I tried, I couldn't overcome these sins on my own. I could say with Paul, "I do not understand what I do. For what I want to do I do not do, but what I hate I do" (Romans 7:15). I tried everything—changing my diet, getting plenty rest, taking daily walks, counting to ten, deep breathing—you name it! Nothing worked. I would still speak harshly or raise my voice at one of my dear little ones when frustrated. I would even wake early every morning to read my Bible, thinking surely the Lord would honor this work of mine and replace my irritable spirit with a calm, peaceful heart.

So, there I sat one morning, utterly devoid of any ability to see past my own sins. I was so angry with myself and fearful of leaving the room lest I raise my voice in anger again. With much effort, I opened my Bible to the Psalms, a place I knew would be sweet solace for me. I turned to Psalm 18 and started to read, "I love you, LORD, my strength. The LORD is my rock, my fortress and my deliverer; my God is my rock, in whom I take refuge, my shield and the horn of my salvation, my stronghold." *Are you really these things to me, O Lord? After all I have done, how my words have hurt my precious children, you are a rock and shield for me?* "I called to the LORD, who is worthy of praise and I have been saved from my enemies." *Lord, this anger within me feels like an enemy; how do I fight it?* "The cords of death entangled me; the torrents of destruction overwhelmed me. The cords of the grave coiled around me; the snares of death confronted me. In my distress I called to the LORD; I cried to my God for help. From his temple he heard my voice; my cry came before him to his ears." *Lord, do you really hear me? Why aren't you helping me?*

The earth trembled and quaked,
and the foundations of the mountains shook;
they trembled because he was angry.
Smoke rose from his nostrils;
consuming fire came from his mouth,

burning coals blazed out of it.
He parted the heavens and came down;
dark clouds were under his feet.
He mounted the cherubim and flew;
He soared on the wings of the wind.
He made darkness his covering, his canopy around him—
the dark rain clouds of the sky.
Out of the brightness of his presence clouds advanced,
with hailstones and bolts of lightning.
The LORD thundered from heaven;
the voice of the Most High resounded.
He shot his arrows and scattered the enemy,
with great bolts of lightning he routed them.
The valleys of the sea were exposed
and the foundations of the earth laid bare
at your rebuke, LORD,
at the blast of breath from your nostrils.

He reached down from on high and took hold of me;
He drew me out of deep waters.
He rescued me from my powerful enemy,
from my foes, who were too strong for me.
They confronted me in the day of my disaster,
but the LORD was my support.
He brought me out into a spacious place;
he rescued me because he delighted in me.

The LORD has dealt with me according to my righteousness;
according to the cleanness of my hands he has rewarded me.
For I have kept the ways of the LORD;
I am not guilty of turning from my God.
All his laws are before me;
I have not turned away from his decrees.
I have been blameless before him
and have kept myself from sin.
The LORD has rewarded me according to my righteousness,
according to the cleanness of my hands in his sight.
To the faithful you show yourself faithful,
to the blameless you show yourself blameless,
to the pure you show yourself pure,
but to the devious you show yourself shrewd.
You save the humble
but bring low those whose eyes are haughty.

You, LORD, keep my lamp burning;
 my God turns my darkness into light.
With your help I can advance against a troop;
 with my God I can scale a wall.
As for God, his way is perfect:
The LORD's word is flawless;
 he shields all who take refuge in him.
For who is God besides the LORD?
And who is the Rock except our God?
It is God who arms me with strength
 and keeps my way secure.
He makes my feet like the feet of a deer;
 he causes me to stand on the heights.
He trains my hands for battle;
 my arms can bend a bow of bronze.
You make your saving help my shield,
 and your right hand sustains me;
 your help has made me great.
You provide a broad path for my feet,
 so that my ankles do not give way.

I pursued my enemies and overtook them;
 I did not turn back till they were destroyed.
I crushed them so that they could not rise;
 they fell beneath my feet.
You armed me with strength for battle;
 you humbled my adversaries before me.
You made my enemies turn their backs in flight,
 and I destroyed my foes.
They cried for help, but there was no one to save them—
 to the LORD, but he did not answer.
I beat them as fine as windblown dust;
 I trampled them like mud in the streets.
You have delivered me from the attacks of the people;
 you have made me the head of nations.
People I did not know now serve me,
 foreigners cower before me;
 as soon as they hear of me, they obey me.
They all lose heart;
 they come trembling from their strongholds.

The LORD lives! Praise be to my Rock!
Exalted be God my Savior!

He is the God who avenges me,
who subdues nations under me,
who saves me from my enemies.
You exalted me above my foes;
from a violent man you rescued me.
Therefore I will praise you, LORD, among the nations;
I will sing the praises of your name.

He gives his king great victories;
he shows unfailing love to his anointed,
to David and to his descendants forever.
-Psalm 18

    I sat there amazed at this, as if reading it for the first time. This God who thunders from the heavens, who can flash forth lightning and lay the foundations of the world bare, He is mighty. This God who makes the mountains tremble is powerful. Yet, in the midst of displaying His might and power, He stoops down to draw me out of many waters, to rescue me from an enemy too strong for me to withstand. This thought flitted across my mind—if God is powerful enough to do all these things, isn't He strong enough to tame my temper? This gave me more hope than I could have ever longed for!
    I was as Christian from Pilgrim's Progress being lifted out of the Slough of Despond by the hand of Help who said, "'Give me thine hand.' So he gave him his hand. So he drew him out and set him upon sound ground and bid him go on his way."[72] I knew I needed help, and I knew I couldn't help myself. I needed someone stronger than me to come along and "bid me go on my way."
    The Lord didn't use "magic" in this time in His Word to take away my anger or to give me a spirit that was never irritable again. Oh, I tried to have my quiet time every morning, hoping it would do the trick and I would have a great day without any irritation, but I soon learned this wasn't how the Lord wanted to use His Word in my life. But this was the beginning of His showing me how powerful His Word was, strengthening me for the battles that lie ahead. God kindly used time in His Word to show me how insidious and pervasive my sin was, "For the word of God is alive and active.

---

[72] *Pilgrim's Progress* by John Bunyan, Moody Publishers, Chicago, 2007 edition by Moody Bible Institute, page 23

Sharper than any double-edged sword, it penetrates even to dividing soul and spirit, joints and of marrow; it judges the thoughts and attitudes of the heart" (Hebrews 4:12). I quickly learned that I needed more than just a quick dose of Scriptures to help me through my day; I needed it to transform my thinking, to shape how I planned our days, to be the words I would speak to others, and so much more.

I am learning to preach the Gospel to myself each day, remembering that, when I trusted Christ as my Lord and Savior, I was a new creation like 2 Corinthians 5:17 says, "Therefore, if anyone is in Christ, the new creation has come: The old has gone, the new is here!" Each day is another day to remember how God has graciously saved me from my sins through the atoning work of Christ on the Cross and, though no work I could ever do would save me (Titus 3:4-7), I still have to walk in obedience and trust each and every day of my life.

Here is a small list of some wonderful lessons I am still learning from God's Word.

It guards us from sin:

How can a young person stay on the path of purity? By living according to your word. I seek you with all my heart; do not let me stray from your commands. I have hidden your word in my heart that I might not sin against you.
-Psalm 119:9-11

It strengthens us when we are weary and battle sore:

God is our refuge and strength, an ever-present help in trouble. Therefore we will not fear though the earth give way and the mountains fall into the heart of the sea, though its waters roar and foam and the mountains quake with their surging.
There is a river whose streams make glad the city of God, the holy place where the Most High dwells. God is within her, she shall not fail; God will help her at break of day
-Psalm 46:1-5

It rebukes and admonishes us:

Blot out my transgressions. Wash away all my iniquity and cleanse me from my sin. For I know my transgressions, and my sin is always before me. Against you, you only, have I sinned and done what is evil in your sight; so you are right in

your verdict and justified when you judge
-Psalm 51:1-4

It gives us reason to rejoice:

There is therefore now no condemnation for those who are in Christ Jesus.
-Romans 8:1

Our home is very different now than it was many years ago. I wish I could say the past eight years have been filled with my speaking only words of grace and encouragement to my precious children, but I have stumbled and fallen, raised my voice far more than I would have liked, apologized to my children, and taught them many lessons in humility and seeking forgiveness. I have learned to be alone and pray before a stressful situation and to walk away quickly, open God's Word, and pray when I feel anger welling up in my heart. I have learned to memorize and meditate on God's Word as much as possible and to place Scripture verses throughout our home to remind me of the strength He alone can provide. As I have done these things, I find myself less and less irritated with the situations around me and far more able to be strengthened to live the life that God intends for me, His struggling pilgrim.

> O to grace how great a debtor
> Daily I'm constrained to be!
> Let Thy goodness, like a fetter,
> Bind my wandering heart to Thee.
> Prone to wander, Lord, I feel it,
> Prone to leave the God I love;
> Here's my heart, O take and seal it,
> Seal it for Thy courts above.[73]

BABY BUS

My transportation is what I call my baby bus for people with disabilities. In Columbus, Ohio, it's called Project Mainstream, and it picks me up at home, takes me to my destination, and brings me home. One day, I was riding the bus going home, and a few blocks away from my house, the driver stopped. I looked and saw what

---

[73] See Appendix: Music Notes

was a likely fender-bender accident. The street was two lanes, and the cars were blocking all traffic. We could not go around because of oncoming traffic. I heard the driver say something like, "Oh my goodness. Look at this." I peered out to see two youngish women pointing fingers at each other and yelling. Their faces revealed so much anger. The bus windows were down, and it was easy to hear their ranting. Believe me, it wasn't nice.

We finally were able to go around them and saw that the cars were not damaged at all. The driver and I spoke rather softly saying that the scene was disheartening and certainly selfish for them to block traffic because they were angry. This kind of angst serves no real purpose. Who would back down first? Who would make amends? If one of the women had been a Christian, how might she have acted differently when the world's anger was flying at her with a pointing finger and foul words? Am I correct in assuming neither were Christians? When I see something like this, I can't help but wonder about the women's lives, how frustrated they must be. Will they bend everyone's ear that evening, and the next few days, about the "horrible woman" who hit her car? And I wonder, too, what I would do in that circumstance.

No one said it's easy to be a Christian, but it is worth it.

The same people after they have broken free from anger might now be feeding off each other's grace, love, forgiveness, and sweet spirit of the Lord. See the difference? If we surround ourselves with people who are free through Christ, we gain the strength to go out in the world to spread the Good News. We have the ability to help others see that breaking free is sweeter when God is our Father, when love reigns and not bitterness, gossip, anger, jealousy, and all the petty human characteristics we need to shed to fly free.

To be free in Christ is a blessing.

Keep one thing in view forever- the truth; and if you do this, though it may seem to lead you away from the opinion of men, it will assuredly conduct you to the throne of God.
-Horace Mann[74]

---

74   See Appendix: Quote References

10

Only God Can Make a Tree

Then God said, 'Let the land produce vegetation: seed-bearing plants and trees on the land that bear fruit with seed in it, according to their various kinds.' And it was so. The land produced vegetation: plants bearing seed according to their kinds and trees bearing fruit with seed in it according to their kinds. And God saw that it was good. And there was evening, and there was morning—the third day
-Genesis 1:11-13

My love of nature has been strong as long as I can remember. My Grandmother Esther Page, whom we called Kaki, had a farm in East Columbus, Ohio originally with more than 700 acres where I spent many hours as a girl exploring, enjoying the sounds and even the quietness of God's gifts to us in nature. Much of my writing has equated the beauty of nature with it being a gift God gave us to learn about him. When I lived in California, in the early 70s, I was driving and enjoying the open land. It was nearly sunset and I stopped to see a spectacular view and wrote the following poem:

The Farmland
(Liz Thompson, 1972)

> The evening sun
> Invites the stranger to trespass,
> To hurdle the fence
> And leave the coolness of life behind.
> Intrigues him to wander
> Beyond --

And experience the wonder
That was lost
When he was
No longer a child.
To smell the hay,
Fresh mown grass and
To await the first evening star with
Breathless anticipation!

When my ability to hear was fading, I realized it through nature sounds. Hearing bird songs, water flowing over rocks, cicadas on a summer night, and the breeze blowing through the trees was always a joy to me. Our family was camping and during one trip I noticed the cicada were so loud they kept me awake. While everyone else snoozed, I tossed and turned in my sleeping bag.

"Ahhh! They stopped," I said to myself as I turned on my other side. Eventually I slept but turned over again.

"Oh no, there they are again!" I mumbled to myself. It took a few turns before the realization came to me that with the one ear, I heard nothing. The cicada didn't simply stop chirping, my right ear was deaf, or as I would soon learn, close to deafness. It hit like a blow to my gut and I was sleepless the rest of the night. I knew my hearing was getting worse, but this experience was so intense I could not ignore it anymore.

In 1996, we lived in Arizona and work was becoming difficult for me to do because secretarial work usually included extensive phone work. I knew nothing of self-advocacy and very little about assistive devices. This fear drove me to beg Bob to move back to Ohio; in the grayest months of Ohio, too, from the most beautiful months in Arizona. I wrote the following poem where I knew God was in control and that my other senses allowed me to enjoy nature.

I Guess I Knew
(Liz Thompson, January 22, 1996)

I guess I knew I'd miss the rain
The gentle patter on the windowpane.
The smell of air so clean and fresh
Like the world had just been washed.
I guess I knew I'd miss the nights
With crickets chirping for all their might.
The humid, warm and misty feel
At night when the sun had lost its zeal.

I guess I knew I'd miss my friends
The faces of people who knew me when.
People who may just say hello
Or how are you, they just want to know.
I guess I knew what I had then
And what I'm going back to again.
The memories are real enough
I haven't glossed it over, I'm still in touch.
I guess I knew the reason we left
To fulfill a dream, to empty a bag
To know again just what we had
And know we want it back again.
I guess I knew God's in control
He knows what it takes to make us whole.
Sometimes to miss, sometimes to gain
To know what we want, to know where we've been.
I guess I knew and now I'm sure
Life is full of dreams galore.
We have to pick so carefully
We must recognize our destiny.
I guess I knew as time went on
That I might never write another song.
But my heart is full and I love my life.
I guess I knew I'd be alright.

On the bright side, my discovery of my worsening hearing led me to realize I needed to get hearing aids. I did this at 39 and 42 and they helped until I was 50 and was completely deaf. After I received my first cochlear implant, which restored more than 95 percent of my hearing and speech clarity, it didn't surprise me that the first sounds that brought tears to my eyes were sounds of nature.

The day my implant was activated, I drove home alone by choice and a storm was in the distance. I retreated to our backyard. The wind blew but was I really hearing it? I followed the sound with the movement of leaves and sure enough, it was the wind I was hearing. Tears of joy sprung to my eyes as next I heard a crow caw-caw-cawing and I laughed! Never have I tired of the sounds of birds, wind, rain on the roof or canvas of our camper, and laughter floating on the wind.

I have lived, a long time, and the longer I live, the more convincing proofs I see of this truth--that God governs in the affairs of men. And if a sparrow cannot fall to the ground without his

notice, is it probable that an empire can rise without his aid?
-Benjamin Franklin

The following was published in Suburban News Publications **August 20, 2007:**

The True Value of 'a bird in the hand'
(Liz Thompson)

Is it that news is all bad or is the good news—the shining moments—hidden from view? We read and hear about bridges collapsing, local and national government corruption or the scent of it, lives ending dramatically and too soon, August heat, fires, floods—well, most of us know the list is endless.

I know many of my friends and family tire of reading and watching news which seems slanted toward disaster and hyped dramas. Many of us crumple the newspapers and magazines in disgust and talk to the newscasters as if they can hear us and end up turning the television off.

Life continues on as we read about and see disaster looming. I'm not naïve—the world is full of danger and disheartening stories. When I was a reporter, I was required to cover local government meetings, police reports and hometown events. My eyes were opened to realities I didn't know existed on the local level. Often I thought problems began "at the top." The foundation of our country, beginning on the small town level, needs to be strong and unsoiled for the "top" to be sturdy.

As time passed as a reporter, I gravitated to the stories of neighborhood people who were living sincere lives in spite of city woes and worldwide disaster. These people I met, and still meet today, live what they believe and spend time passing on the qualities of life they feel make the world a better place to live.

Recently, a small sparrow zoomed into our patio door with a thud I heard in the next room. I found the bird lying belly up on the doorstep and carefully opened the door to inspect. I scooped the bird into the palm of my hand and sat down in a nearby chair. The bird's eyes were open and moving. He was so light and soft – downy describes how it felt in my hand – and I gently stroked its small head while talking to it.

He let me move his legs and he blinked his eyes as I talked. Obviously, the bird was stunned by the conk on its head and would revive soon. I took a drop of water from our dog's water dish and dropped it on the beak. The still body shook, turned over and took flight. He would survive and join the other birds.

The song, "His Eye is on the Sparrow" (and I know He watches me), ran in my head. I know God watches over us but this song became real in a moment.

This is small news. A few moments in the life of one person. But to me it was good news. It brightened my day and I could feel the fluff of the bird's feathers in my palm for a long time that day and once again as I write about the moment he lay in my hand.

Life is fragile. In a moment we could be somewhere where the earth or man-made object collapses underneath us. I'm not being fatalistic but realistic. Not one of us knows the number of days we will be on this earth. Just like the small bird, we ram our heads into objects, real or surreal, every day trying to get ahead, make a living, pay the bills, clean the house, shop for food, raise our children, keep or improve our health—whatever takes up each of our 24-hour daytime spans.

We could sure use a lift now and again by someone who is willing to hold our persona long enough that we can revive, gain our senses and go our way in the world. We could sure use more good news to balance out the negativity in the world.

Maybe the store clerk who has been on his or her feet all day could use a smile or word of appreciation. Or the driver who lets us into the flow of traffic could use a wave and a smile of thanks. When our family returns home today, a hug and "I'm glad you're home" or "I missed you" would help his or her evening be lighter. A few words, a smile, a hug or somehow letting another person know they matter in your life will make the bad news bearable one more day. And just maybe, if the foundation of the small places is positive and sturdy, the larger picture will grow brighter. One person at a time.

Look for the moments. They exist and are as soft as that small bird was in my hand.

{end}

This poem may knock you over with a feather:

Overheard in an Orchard
(Elizabeth Chaney, 1859)

Said the Robin to the Sparrow:
"I should really like to know
Why these anxious human beings
Rush about and worry so."

Said the Sparrow to the Robin,
"Friend, I think that it must be
That they have no heavenly Father,
Such as cares for you and me."

The simplicity of sparrows obviously amazes me. There are so many of them yet God watches over each one. I love the song, "His eye is on the sparrow" by Civilla D. Martin:

Why should I be discouraged,
Why should the shadows fall
Why should my heart be lonely
And long for Heaven and Home.
When Jesus is my portion
My constant friend is He
His eye is on the sparrow
And I know He watches me.
His eye is on the sparrow,
And I know He watches me. (Full lyrics in Music Notes)

Some may look at the Sparrow as a nuisance or messy bird but I like its plainness and the fact it doesn't stand out with a bright color like a Cardinal or Goldfinch. The Sparrow represents the majority, in my thinking, like us. And God knows every single one, just like He knows each of us. I have held a sparrow in my hand and it was soft, small and detailed more than we can see in a group of them. When some active Sparrows built a huge nest in the top of our front porch, I enjoyed watching how hard they worked to get into the area. They had to enter upside down. It amazed me! This year, when Bob replaced the post and had to clear out the nest, it filled half of a paper lawn bag. Many sparrows had been living there and kept coming back for weeks after their home was destroyed looking for a way to enter their nest to no avail. I prayed, and knew, that God would find them another home for the winter.

I have had many sparrow friends watching out for me as God's children. We need each other to encourage, direct and travel on our flight through life with us.

Joyce Kilmer's poem, Trees, is known by many:

Trees
(Joyce Kilmer [1886-1918])

I THINK that I shall never see

A poem lovely as a tree.
A tree whose hungry mouth is prest
Against the earth's sweet flowing breast;
A tree that looks at God all day,
And lifts her leafy arms to pray;
A tree that may in Summer wear
A nest of robins in her hair;
Upon whose bosom snow has lain;
Who intimately lives with rain.
Poems are made by fools like me,
But only God can make a tree.

("Trees" was originally published in *Trees and Other Poems*. Joyce Kilmer. New York: George H. Doran Company, 1914.)

As a child, the only air conditioning was open windows and fans. Since I was born with red hair, freckles were part of my complexion from the first time I was in the sun. On my grandmother's farm, a family by the name of Woods lived on the land and tended the cows, chickens, pigs and whatever was there. Kaki always had a vegetable garden. One summer, we were weeding and picking produce from the garden when a brush fire started. I was very young but thought I could help. My Mom sent me to the house with my grandmother. I remember she held me in the cane-woven chair she had by her telephone in her breakfast room. She tried to explain why I couldn't help. (Too young, might hurt myself, etc.) I could see the smoke out the tall, wide windows and wondered why I couldn't help.

This chair where we sat is where I always visualized her when she called or I called her. Now I'm a grandmother and pray I'm leaving good memories in the lives of my grandchildren. My granddaughter, Elizabeth, has become a writer with a true love of nature and the beauty surrounding her each day. The following is one poem she has written, among many, followed by one I wrote of a similar nature.

Dusk
(Elizabeth Dunkel at age 10)

Under the shade of a tree,
With crickets chirping close by,
The cool sweet evening darkens,
And the end of the day draws nigh.
Birds sing a final sweet song,
The scent of the herbs-parsley and mint,

The soft green clover swaying in the breeze,
The bright setting sun with its warm golden tint,
The end of the day draws nigh,
And the earth says a final, "Goodbye."

True Grace?
(Liz Thompson)

    Blue sky all above me
    And the air is cold, yet not harsh.
    The silence is a wonder,
    A peace as golden as the sun.
    It warms me in the evening
    When the sunlight rays are gone.
    As I walk the meadow
    And gaze wistfully towards the sky
    A smile is close and in my heart
    But sometimes yet, I cry.
    The tears of life are salty
    And feel cold upon my face.
    Yet I often wonder
    If they are signs of God's true grace.
    (January 6, 1997)

Spending time on my grandmother's farm holds many treasured memories. The women were all knitters; my grandmother, Esther Page, my Mother, Mary Day, my aunts, Esther Starr, Eva Page and Pam Page. Many nights, while we children - my brothers Jim and Jon Day, my sister Cynthia (Slocum), and sometimes one or more of my cousins Tom Page, Susan, Rachel (Radin), and Ricky Starr, and Francey (Porter) and Walter Page - played while the women knitted on the screened porch and the men chatted. I remember candles glowing while laughter and talk floated on the night breeze. Many a time, I fell asleep on the large, cushioned porch swing just listening to the talking and sounds of summer. This poem speaks to many of these memories.

September Night Play
(Liz Thompson)
September 1988

    One stitch at a time,
    A loop and a knot,

Twist and a turn,
A pattern not forgot.
Knitting needles clicking
And conversation humming,
The citronella candle
And the swing gently bumping.
Lightening bugs and laughter
And children running after
With a jar and lid with holes punched through
To let the captured breathe air, too.
"Put on a sweater,
It's getting late."
Darkness and coolness
Do not hesitate.
The Weeping Willow
Is a grand hiding place!
But it is time to go home
And end our night play.
Only wishing that
We could stay
But school comes tomorrow,
Another autumn day.
So good-bye to Grandma
She must return to her porch.
One stitch at a time,
A loop and a knot.
Twist and a turn
A pattern not forgot.
Who will have a new sweater
To keep them warm at night.
While catching bugs in a jar
To watch their green,
Glowing light?
I'm sleepy – goodnight.

I believe in God like I believe in the sun rise. Not because I can see it, but because I can see all that it touches.
-C. S. Lewis

When I hear of other butterfly moments, I am always stunned how the simplicity of a butterfly holds such a powerful message.

**Glorious Answer in Living Color
(Kathleen Welty)
*Names have been changed.**

Nightmares begin with what kinds of scenes? Envision your 21-year-old child, your first-born, and your only son, crushed on the street in a motorcycle wreck. He was hit by a car and did not regain consciousness. He was pronounced "brain dead" at the hospital. Imagine that this horrifying scene had been preceded by nightmares which featured the death of two siblings, the estrangement of family members, and the close-up view of a spouse's infidelity followed by a divorce you did not want. You would not imagine this if you were Sheila*. It was her reality.

Sheila and I crossed paths when her son Trevor* was in kindergarten. I became his baby-sitter and my oldest son became his playmate. Though we were neighbors for just three years, our bond was fastened tight because we cared deeply for one another. She weathered the storms in her marriage during the years we shared property lines. On my side of the fence there was a shrub line that kept her safe from the sadness within her house. In our yard was an old-fashioned wooden lawn swing whose comfortable benches allowed us to watch our children roam and play nearby. It was the kind of swing that had two seats facing one another—a great boon to intimate conversation. Its slow back-and-forth sway worked a soothing magic.

We sat there many times during those three summers, even in the spring and autumn when other less hearty individuals would have stayed inside. Our sons loved the outdoors, too, and were glad their mommies liked to visit. My husband worked double shifts and therefore, I, too, had time for deep conversations.

Both Sheila and I had a steadfast faith in Christ, believed that prayer changed things, and relied on the Bible for guidance. In the midst of that knowledge we sometimes floundered for hope. Often we grasped vainly for understanding when Sheila was blindsided by yet another family crisis.

How I ached for Sheila! Her marriage spiraled downward with no resolution in sight. But she refused to be kicked into the pit of despair. She suffered many heartaches that threatened to undo her resolve; which was always love the man to whom she had pledged her life. Even when he divorced her, even when the "other woman's" mother (supposedly a Christian woman) vocalized her joy that her daughter had "caught a rich one this time," even when Sheila's single-mom income stretched to its limit, she kept her sanity. Some would say 'I don't know how she did it,' but I do. She had faith.

This is not to say she never gave into the sorrow. When she was tempted to throw away all hope, Jesus heard the gasp of her prayer. He drew near, and Sheila was spared from horror that the devil offered her, wrapped in a package that covered its evil contents.

By the time our sons had become college-age I had been away from Sheila's neighborhood for 15 years. We had remained tied at the heartstrings though Sheila and I seldom visited anymore. Yet when I heard about Trevor's death, I knew I needed to be at the funeral. The 150-mile trip took on a surreal quality. Alone with my memories, this present day reality would not sink in. When I walked into the funeral home, saw the plastic white letters that spelled Trevor James Young on the directional sign, my insides shook. I had to acknowledge that another of Sheila's nightmares was real.

After the funeral, Sheila phoned me. We had not had an opportunity connect and she had much on her mind. We couldn't sit on that swing and talk, because it was on my backyard patio, just outside the door of our walkout basement. How I longed for Sheila to come and rest there with me, so I could somehow try to help her through this mire of grief in a tangible way. A telephone conversation would have to do.

"I have to ask you something and I don't bring it up with many people," Sheila said. "I raised Trevor to love Jesus and I know when he was young he was excited about his relationship with Christ…" Her voice trailed off. She cleared her throat and continued. "It was during his teen years that he stayed more with his dad and his priorities changed. His friends were not Christians, and he had little interest in his spiritual life. You remember those hard times we went through." She paused. "But you know, Kathy, it was just recently that he talked to me about changes he wanted to make in his lifestyle. He owned up to the mistakes he had made during those years. But we never quite finished that conversation."

Sheila fought back tears and we talked about Trevor's kind heart and his genuine love for his family.

"Kathy, this is what I've been wondering. During those two days when Trevor was pronounced brain-dead, his heart was beating and I agonized about his spiritual life at that point. I wondered if his soul was there—because I knew if it was, he knew how to pray. He knew how to get his priorities lined up. He understood repentance, he believed in God the Father, God the Son and God the Holy Spirit. Do you have any insights?"

I recall that my answer came slowly. I was thinking and praying and talking to Sheila all at the same time. I didn't know what to say. I wanted my reply to offer a lifeline, not mindless or flippant words. This was heavy.

"I'm not well-versed on such things. But I know God would honor Trevor's deepest desire to serve Him. You know, Sheila, I'm not going to say I'm an expert, but I have a feeling we're going to somehow know the real answer to your question. Somehow. I think the gut-level honest answer will come as we pray."

I paused and the line was silent a moment. "I trust you, Kathy," Sheila said. And our heartstrings grew stronger.

After we said our good-byes, I replaced the phone on its base, turned to my left and took three steps to our main-floor window that overlooked our patio below. I was deep in contemplation and praying for guidance to know how to help Sheila. My eyes stared out then suddenly focused, for that very swing where Sheila and I had knit our strong friendship was directly below me. I was drawn to stare at it, remembering those hours of conversations. Only ten or fifteen seconds passed when a beautiful butterfly flitted into my visual range, then landed directly in front of me, on the top of this swing. My birds-eye view of the butterfly gave me a spectacular view of its widespread wings—almost as if it had practiced its best pose. I had never seen one like it before. It was a marvelous light blue, both on its top set of wings and the bottom set. It had a thin outline of black, but no other colors were on its wings. It took my breath away. A split-second of amazement at its beauty turned into a solid understanding that the prayer of my heart was answered as I hung up the phone between Sheila and me. That butterfly had been on its mission even then as it flew toward my backyard.

The beautiful butterfly stayed on the top of the swing for several minutes while I worshiped God in silence. I knew this was His answer to Sheila. I knew the swing was the best place for me to understand the message. I knew that I knew that I knew. I called Sheila.

And I was ecstatic. Though the long miles between us kept us apart, we were together in praise for God's certain and immediate answer. When I described the butterfly to her in detail, she gasped. "Trevor's favorite color, his whole life, was light blue!" Her voice revealed newfound joy.

I've not seen a butterfly like it since that day. I don't think I ever will, because I'm convinced it was created for that mission.

After a search on the Internet, I found some interesting facts about butterflies and insects in general. I copied these from www.thebutterflysite.com

Fun Butterfly Facts:[75]

1. Butterflies range in size from a tiny 1/8 inch to a huge almost 12 inches.
2. Butterflies can see red, green, and yellow.
3. Some people say that when the black bands on the Wooly bear caterpillar are wide, a cold winter is coming.
4. The top butterfly flight speed is 12 miles per hour. Some moths can fly 25 miles per hour!
5. Monarch butterflies journey from the Great Lakes to the Gulf of Mexico, a distance of about 2,000 miles, and return to the north again in the spring.
6. Butterflies cannot fly if their body temperature is less than 86 degrees.
7. Representations of butterflies are seen in Egyptian frescoes at Thebes, which are 3,500 years old.
8. Antarctica is the only continent on which no Lepidoptera have been found.
9. There are about 24,000 species of butterflies. The moths are even more numerous: about 140,000 species of them were counted all over the world.
10. The Brimstone butterfly (Gonepterix rhamni) has the longest lifetime of the adult butterflies: 9-10 months.
11. Some Case Moth caterpillars (Psychidae) build a case around themselves that they always carry with them. It is made of silk and pieces of plants or soil.
12. The caterpillars of some Snout Moths (Pyralididae) live in or on water-plants.
13. The females of some moth species lack wings, all they can do to move is crawl.
14. The Morgan's Sphinx Moth from Madagascar has a proboscis (tube mouth) that is 12 to 14 inches long to get the nectar from the bottom of a 12 inch deep orchid discovered by Charles Darwin.

---

75   http://www.thebutterflysite.com/facts.shtml

15. Some moths never eat anything as adults because they don't have mouths. They must live on the energy they stored as caterpillars.
16. Many butterflies can taste with their feet to find out whether the leaf they sit on is good to lay eggs on to be their caterpillars' food or not.
17. There are more types of insects in one tropical rain forest tree than there are in the entire state of Vermont.
18. In 1958 Entomologist W.G. Bruce published a list of Arthropod references in the Bible. The most frequently named bugs from the Bible are: Locust: 24, Moth: 11, Grasshopper: 10, Scorpion: 10, Caterpillar: 9, and Bee: 4.
19. People eat insects – called "Entomophagy"(people eating bugs) – it has been practiced for centuries throughout Africa, Australia, Asia, the Middle East, and North, Central and South America. Why? Because many bugs are both protein-rich and good sources of vitamins, minerals and fats.
20. YOU can eat bugs! Try the "Eat-A-Bug Cookbook" by David George Gordon , 10 Speed Press. Don't want to cook them yourself? Go to HotLix for all sorts of insect goodies! My favorites are "Cricket-lickit's" – a flavored sucker with a real edible cricket inside.
21. Many insects can carry 50 times their own body weight. This would be like an adult person lifting two heavy cars full of people.
22. There are over a million described species of insects. Some people estimate there are actually between 15 and 30 million species.
23. Most insects are beneficial to people because they eat other insects, pollinate crops, are food for other animals, make products we use (like honey and silk) or have medical uses.
24. Butterflies and insects have their skeletons on the outside of their bodies, called the exoskeleton. This protects the insect and keeps water inside their bodies so they don't dry out.

The ocean holds many wonderful gifts. When I listen to the ocean surf rolling in, there is little else I want to hear. It's soothing and continuous. Something I can count on. The waves of the sea roll in on shore twenty-six to the minute in all kinds of weather.

How comforting to know that God was consistent in His planning the world and he is our absolute. I have been fortunate to live in California, Seattle and Arizona. The best part of living in California and Seattle was the nearness of the ocean. In Santa Barbara, California, I was a 10-minute bike ride from the beach. Seattle's ocean views were rockier and much colder but no less spectacular. This following poem was written after we lived in the Seattle area and had visited Deception Pass State Park on Whidbey Island in Northern Washington.

Not Alone, but Free
(Liz Thompson)

>I have been to the ocean
>At least once, it seems
>And I relive it in my dreams.
>The surf's so loud
>It drowns all thoughts,
>The seagulls fly above and squawk.
>the endless waves roll on and on
>Like a rhythmic, children's song.
>Sand castles wash away again
>As the tide rolls up and sinks them in.
>On the horizon, islands lie,
>A lovely blessing for one's eye.
>White puffs of clouds
>Float in an azure sky
>And the air is so fresh
>It could make one cry.
>Laughter cannot be heard, but seen
>Like hopes relived
>From another dream.
>The darkness comes -
>Night has arrived
>the clouds have vanished
>And stars light the sky
>Like hundreds of flashlights
>Filtering down
>To this sandy, cold and watery ground.
>The moon appears
>Like the mother light
>Guarding her stars
>From the dark of night.
>As the waves roll ashore

In their lilting song,
I drift into slumber
That may not last long.
For what are dreams?
But our hopes relived -
that we long to share
And so live,
As one would hope our dreams to be -
Long, with love
Not alone, but free.
(September 1988)

God gives us so many gifts every day like the sounds and beauty of nature, laughter, food, shelter, clothing, friends, and more. One morning I was awake early as the sun was rising. Looking out the window I noticed our large hibiscus flower blooms were curled inward. I didn't realize they closed at night. As the sun awoke and spread its light, the blooms opened to greet it, showing the colors inside. I like to think the blooms were waking up to the sun or Son and so can we. We rest or sleep but when the light of the Son shines, we open up and smile, greeting each new day.

In 2001, while I was a reporter for *Suburban News Publications*, I was on the road often. Since I could not do phone interviews, due to my profound hearing loss, I drove to every interview; which in the long run proved more interesting and honest in my reporting. After years of sitting in offices or cubicles as a secretary, the freedom was a blessing I never took for granted or abused. I loved driving with the windows down while taking in the changing seasons of Ohio. I started out loving nature and I'm sure that love led me to my love of God and his Son, Jesus. Recently, we had the first light snowfall of the season. I stepped out and saw the white flakes gathering on my little black dog's fur. "Oh, it's snowing!" I exclaimed. I chuckled remembering a column I wrote years ago when I wrote of a similar experience. I picked up the phone and dialed my daughter and my grandson, Andrew answered.

"Hi, Andrew. How are you today?" I started.

"Good here, Nana."

"It's snowing here! Is it there?" I asked excited.

"No it's sunny and bright here. It's snowing there??" he said with a smile.

"Just a little but I had to share it with someone. Get your sleds ready!" I laughed.

"OK, Nana, but it's a little early," he pondered.

"I love you, Andrew. Watch for the snow!" and I rang off.

Then less than a month later, I awoke to an answering machine message from Andrew.

"Nana, it's me, Andrew. It's REALLY snowing here! I just wanted to let you know!"

What grandmother would ignore that message? Not this one. I called and left a message for him.

"Andrew, thank you for the call! It is snowing here, too, and I really think you should polish your sleds."

Later, he called and we connected talking about the snow and how pretty it was and that yes, they still had their sleds and would be getting ready. What joy these conversations hold for me.

Here is a portion of the column I wrote and was published January 24, 2001 in *Suburban News Publications*.

Hope Floats When You're Doing Something You Love (Liz Thompson)

I stepped outside into the wind of early winter and snow fell lightly. I exclaimed aloud, "The first snow!" and felt almost foolish. I just laughed and kept my face toward the falling snow. Smiling, I hoped I would never lose that childlike wonder of things like the first snow. Christmas morning, and old song.

Watching the movie *Hope Floats* again, my favorite dialog was being spoken and I knew I must write about this. The main male character, Justin Matisse, is talking with his romantic counterpart, Birdee Pruitt. He is a gifted craftsman and she is admiring his beautiful home that he designed and was building himself. Birdee asks why he goes around town painting houses when he could do so much more? Justin laughs, saying that she is talking about the American Dream, right? Then he says, "I know what you mean. You start out loving something, you twist it and torture it trying to make money at it. You spend a lifetime doing that and at the end you can't find a trace of what you started out loving." He asks her what she started out loving and she can't remember. I thought about it. What did I start out loving in this life? ...

As the blustery wind blew my hair today, I was not bothered. Then it hit me that I have always loved being outdoors and writing about it--in forest areas, near a lake or ocean, during any season but especially spring and autumn when the air is particularly fresh. I remember the first spring after one of my grandmothers died. I was sitting outside crying, thinking how she would have loved the day's weather: sunny, cool and a clear, blue sky. My mind was filled with memories of walking down her lane to get her mail while she would quietly sign at a beautiful day, in no hurry. Is it genetic? This love of nature?

Our parents used to take us on "Sunday drives" after church. Westerville (Ohio) was a village in those days and heading to the country was a drive of just a few minutes. We would come to a hill and at the top, it was almost inevitable for Dad to say, "Ohhhh, look at that!" It might have been trees, a lake, a flock of birds, cows, sheep or any variety of nature's wonders spread before us. I don't think I appreciated it outwardly as a youngster but I remember agreeing privately that whatever it was, it was worth the oooooing and ahhhhing.

I started out loving the outdoors. Fresh air--sheets hung to dry outside that smelled like fresh air making sleep more restful--camping and sleeping in open fields under a moonlit sky, breathing the air that we are gifted to enjoy. At Girl Scout camp, everything smelled of canvas (usually wet) and wood. These memories are easily awakened with the familiar scents.

When I was 13, our scouting unit slept at the edge of a wooded area on pine needles for mattresses. I remember waking and seeing two deer lying next to me! I moved and, naturally, they ran away. It seemed like a dream at the time, but the other girls saw the deer as well.

Maybe that is why I bought Save the Rain Forest coffee beans from the Arbor Day Website. I sure didn't need another coffee mug, but it was a small way of saving what I love--nature in its purist, simplest form.

As a child of the 50s, our entertainment was running, playing tag, skating, biking, mowing grass with push mowers -- well I remember it as entertainment) and swimming. At night we would wash our dirty, bare feet before climbing into bed with its fresh-air sheets awaiting us. There was no air-conditioning in homes, we slept with windows open and an old fan lulled us to sleep.

I started out loving pure nature. It is still a wonder to me, daily. As I recycle and use cloth napkins and rags, I hope to save a tree doing what I can to pass on some memories to the following generations.

What did you start out loving?
{end of column}

Reading this again, I pray my Grandmother Page is in heaven

enjoying the beauty of nature, one of her great loves on earth. I am comforted knowing that God has prepared a place for each of us in heaven, if we believe in his Son, Jesus. My imagination can do no justice to what God has prepared for each of us but I am hoping it will be a home in the out of doors where I can gather in all the love God placed in his creation.

Rhythm
(Liz Thompson)
February 5, 2000

>Winter sky
>Glows soft peach
>Early morning.
>White frozen rain
>In mounds abundantly.
>Icicles cling for life
>Dripping rhythmically
>To oblivion.
>Small birds hover
>In barren brush
>Anticipating spring,
>Soft ground,
>Blue sky and warm sun.
>Seeds pushing new growth
>Through dark soil.
>For now--
>Anticipation is a gift
>In itself.
>(February 5, 2000)

Each new day we must thank God for the beauty he gave us in nature. "The heavens declare the glory of God; the skies proclaim the work of his hands."
-Psalm 19:1.

Some marvelous wonders of this world are shared with us if we take the time to see and learn. What an awesome and orderly God we have.[76]

- The eggs of the potato bug hatch in 7 days;

---

76   http://www.ourfullhouse.com/18-daily-life/397-god-of-order.html

- Those of the canary in 14 days;
- Those of the barnyard hen in 21 days;
- The eggs of ducks and geese hatch in 28 days;
- Those of the mallard in 35 days;
- The eggs of the parrot and ostrich hatch in 42 days.

All are divisible by seven, the number of days in a week. God's wisdom is revealed in his arrangement of sections and segments, as well as the number of grains:

- Each watermelon has an even number of stripes on the rind.
- Each orange has an even number of segments.
- Each ear of corn has an even number of grains.
- Every bunch of bananas has on its lowest row an even number of bananas, and each row decreases by one, so that one row has an even number and the next row an odd number.
- The waves of the sea roll in on shore twenty-six to the minute in all kinds of weather.
- All grains are found in even numbers on the stalks, and the Lord specified thirty-fold, sixty-fold, and a hundred-fold - all even numbers.

God has caused the flowers to blossom at certain specified times during the day, so that Linnaeus, the great botanist, once said that if he had a conservatory containing the right kind of soil, moisture and temperatures, he could tell the time of day or night by the flowers that were open and those what were closed.

So we need not worry when we turn our lives over to God for His care. He has ordered each of our lives in a beautiful way for His glory. Only God, who made the brain and the heart, can successfully guide them to a profitable end. Only the God-planned life is successful--only the life given over to the care of the Lord is fulfilled.

11

Inconvenience or Opportunity?

Don't judge each day by the harvest you reap, but by the seeds you plant.
-Robert Louis Stevenson[77]

The following is a sermon I heard Stan Kirtlan give, and I knew the message was a good one for my book. It speaks to how everyday occurrences can change the course of our life, or day, if we are willing to listen and look for the good in everything God places in our path.

Interruptions
(Stan Kirtlan[78])

Several years ago, I was driving along I-70 in Indiana when a rear tire on my red 1980 Chevette blew. At that high speed, my tire just disintegrated. As a college student on the way to a weekend youth ministry, I was very concerned about how to pay for the repair. I had no money. I had no credit card. And as I was changing the tire, I was angry about this interruption in my day and in my budget. Apparently, there was something on the road because, by the time I had gotten my tire changed, two other cars had pulled their cars over near me. Both of them were very nice cars (as opposed to my "beater") driven by older ladies. As I was placing the rim of my wheel in the hatchback, they both came and asked me to change their tires. A few minutes later, we noticed that traffic was backing up to a standstill on the freeway, and a truck driver sitting on the

---

77   See Appendix: Quote References
78   See Appendix: Contributor Biographies

highway told us that, a few miles up the road, there had been a serious accident involving two large trucks and three cars. One of the ladies said, "I wonder if we didn't have flat tires if one of us might have been in that accident?"

The ladies both insisted on paying me for my help. I tried to resist, but they insisted. After that, I only needed a few dollars to get the new tire for my car. But I still believe that the greatest blessing was God possibly keeping me out of that accident or just giving me the opportunity to help two, very sweet ladies. I had over an hour to wonder on this as I sat in traffic.

Since then, I have always wondered how many "interruptions" are really just part of God's design. Jesus was interrupted often during His ministry. What if those interruptions were just annoyances? A leper stopping Him on His way to a sermon, a hemorrhaging woman on the way to another healing, a mourning mother while He was on His way to rest and teach His disciples—these were all great moments of His ministry. Jesus took advantage of every interruption. I wonder how we can learn to do the same. How can we learn to look for God's purpose in life's interruptions?

The Apostle Paul tells us, in Ephesians 5:16, that we are to be "making the most of every opportunity." Before we do that, we really need to have our eyes open to see God's opportunity in our inconveniences.

What does life look like through the eyes of Christ? How much have we missed by looking at life through our selfish eyes instead of looking at the world through His eyes? John 14:12 says, "Very truly I tell you, whoever believes in me will do the works I have been doing, and they will do even greater things than these, because I am going to the Father."

In a scene from the movie Rocky, Rocky is well into a fight when he sits down with a face that is all bloody and eyes that are swollen shut. He tells his trainer, "I see three of them." His trainer says, "Pick the one in the middle!" It's not always that easy, is it? Often we are sidetracked with double vision, going through life, knowing what we ought to do but choosing to do something else. This sidetracks our effectiveness in ministry. We need to find, like Jesus found, a laser-like focus aimed at understanding what God has placed us here to do, what God has placed us in this community and this church to accomplish. Jesus' focus was laser-like. He had the opportunity to be king at one point, but He walked away from that opportunity, walked away from the people, and went somewhere else where people understood that to be made king at this point in His ministry would have sidetracked His purpose. Over and over again, Jesus had opportunities that He passed up, so He could take advantage of those opportunities that were more valuable and more important. Jesus said He came to seek and save those who were lost. In Mark chapter one, Peter and some of the other apostles came to Jesus, who had been praying all night long, and said, "Everyone is looking for you!" Only the day before, He had healed several people, and the people wanted Him to set up a clinic. He said, "Let us go somewhere else—to the nearby villages—so I can preach there also. That is why I have come." Jesus didn't allow things to sidetrack Him nor did He allow Peter's lack of vision to keep Him from seeing what was most important. We have a lot of examples of Christ focusing on His mission in the Bible. Luke 4:14 was the beginning of Jesus' ministry. He went to Nazareth, His hometown, took a scroll, and began to read it. The Bible actually says that this was His custom, going to the synagogue, so this was something He did often.

On this particular day, He took a passage of Scripture. What He reads doesn't show His determination but what He says after He reads that gives greater understanding of His laser-like focus. Scripture says, "Jesus returned to Galilee in the power of the Spirit, and news about him spread through the whole countryside. He was teaching in their synagogues, and everyone praised him. He went to Nazareth where he had been brought up, and on the Sabbath he went into the synagogue, as was his custom. He stood up to read, and the scroll of the prophet Isaiah was handed to him. Unrolling it, he found the place where it is written: 'The Spirit of the Lord is on me, because he has anointed me to proclaim good news to the poor. He has sent me to proclaim freedom for the prisoners and recover sight for the blind, to set the oppressed free, to proclaim the year of the Lord's favor.' Then he rolled up the scroll, gave it back to the attendant and sat down. The eyes of everyone in the synagogue were fastened on him. He began by saying to them, 'Today this scripture is fulfilled in your hearing'" (Luke 4:14-21).

Let's get back to the prophecy in Isaiah. The fulfillment was in the message that Jesus had come here to bring, "to preach good news to the poor, He has sent me to proclaim freedom to the prisoners, and recover sight to the blind, to release the oppressed, to proclaim the year of the Lord's favor." Jesus understood what His mission was, and He wasn't going to let interruptions sidetrack Him along the way. He would never allow Himself to do anything that would take away from His ministry.

We can walk through our lives using only our selfish eyes and not do anything about the hurts and needs of those around us, or we can choose to look at life through Christ's eyes and do what we can to help others.

Jesus did this constantly. The first time Peter came to Jesus (John 1), Jesus saw something in Peter that he could not see in himself. Jesus said, "Hey Simon, I'm going to change your name to Peter which means rock." Jesus saw something in Peter that other people could not see. In John chapter four, Jesus is with the Samaritan woman. Practically a prostitute, this woman was not of good repute or character and was embarrassed by her own life. Yet Jesus saw something in her that not even the disciples could see. When the disciples came back, they said, "Why is he talking to that woman?" because they didn't see her the way Jesus saw her.

Four chapters later, in John chapter eight, we find the woman who was caught in adultery. In that passage of Scripture, everyone sees a condemned woman—but not Jesus. Jesus sees a life worth saving. He sees someone who needs a friend, a person who needs someone to stick up for her for once in her life. And Jesus did so. He didn't condemn her but sent her on her way and told her to sin no more. Earlier, in chapter seven, Jesus was at a Pharisee's house having dinner, and a woman of poor reputation came and began to anoint Jesus' feet. The Pharisees started murmuring amongst themselves and saying things like, if you really knew what kind of woman this was, you wouldn't want to let her touch you. Jesus corrected them right away and told a wonderful parable about who would love the master most—the one who was forgiven a little or the one who was forgiven a whole bunch. And then He said, "Let this story about this woman coming in to anoint my feet be told everywhere the Gospel is preached." Jesus saw past the sin. He saw past the weaknesses in people, and He saw into their hearts and understood their need of forgiveness and love.

In Luke 12, Jesus was watching people come into the temple and pass the offering box. The Bible tells us that, when many people came to the offering box in the temple, they would intentionally use heavier coins worth very little because it would make a lot of noise when it was put in the offering box. Then a poor woman, who had nothing, tried to sneak over to the box and put in two little copper coins, embarrassed because that was all that she had. But who was it that Jesus praised that day? He didn't praise all of the big shots that dropped their big bags of gold and silver into the box but the poor woman who put in everything she had. Jesus saw things differently. He didn't allow His judgment to be clouded by what everyone else was thinking.

And then in chapter nineteen, there was a short man in Jericho by the name of Zacchaeus. Nobody liked this man; in fact, everyone thought he was the worst of characters because he was a tax collector. Zacchaeus had climbed up a tree to be able to see Jesus, and, when Jesus came by, He said, "Zacchaeus come on down, I'm going to your house. Let's do lunch," Or at least, that's my rendition of it. Zacchaeus came down out of the tree, knowing everyone was thinking, "Of all the places in Jericho, why is Jesus going to have lunch with Zacchaeus? That tells you right there that this man can't be a prophet. If He were a prophet, He would know what kind of man Zacchaeus was!" Jesus knew what kind of man Zacchaeus was. Zacchaeus was chosen for the lunch stop that day because Jesus saw people through different lenses. I want to encourage you to use the same lenses that Jesus used, to see people who Jesus touched, whose lives He changed, whose lives He saved. We have the same opportunity as Jesus did, and He even said, "Anyone who has faith in me will do what I have been doing." What was Jesus doing? He was looking into the lives and hearts of people without judgment but with grace, love, and mercy. In John 15:16-17, He said, "You did not choose me, but I chose you and I appointed you to go and bear fruit; fruit that will last and the Father will give you whatever you ask in my name.

Sometimes we wonder why our prayers are not being answered, but the reason may be that we're not doing what Jesus told us to do. The promise that He will give us what we ask in His name is a conditional promise based on our ability to bear fruit—fruit that will last. Jesus didn't choose us to only come and worship, but He chose us to go and bear fruit. In the Great Commission, Jesus said, "All authority in heaven and earth has been given to me--therefore, go and make disciples." Jesus never wanted us to sit in our little church buildings with their padded little chairs and wait for people to come to us. He said all through scripture to go. We are to go into the highways and byways, to search in every alley and corner for people who have needs, and to look at their lives through the eyes of Jesus, through the lenses He puts on us when we become Christians.

In John 15:8, Jesus said, "This is for my Father's glory that you bear much fruit, showing yourselves to be my disciples." Being a disciple of Jesus means denying yourself and taking up the cross daily. It means we become more and more like Jesus every day that we live. Yet if a church in America were asked, "If your church ceased to exist, would anyone notice?", oftentimes the answer would have to be no because we have made it all about us. If we are to put on these spiritual glasses, we must think differently. We need to think in a different order. Often when we see someone in need, we think the worst first. But we don't see Jesus doing that.

We must believe in serving over being served. In Romans 12:3, it says, "For by the grace given me I say to every one of you: Do not think of yourself more highly than you ought, but rather think of yourself with sober judgment, in accordance with the faith God has distributed to each of you." The church is sometimes accused of having a self-righteous attitude; maybe that is a result of what we have communicated. Though, I hope our lives are lived better than those who do not know Jesus. I hope our faith in Christ makes us better people but not judgmental people. In 1 Corinthians chapter six, the apostle Paul gives a long list of sins: sexual immorality, idolatry, homosexuality, thievery, and all kinds of other sins. Then Paul says, "and that's what some of you were." When we look through the eyes of Jesus, we have something He didn't have. He couldn't relate to them as sinners because He'd always been perfect, sinless.

One thing I know for sure about myself is that I am a sinner saved by the grace of God. My heart needs to break for those people who are simply sinners. I am not any better, and that's why Paul said, "don't think more highly of yourself than you ought to think." That's why he said in Philippians chapter two, "Put other needs ahead of your own." This is how we plant seeds.

Bearing fruit is better than consuming it. I had a banana for breakfast which was delicious, but God didn't put me here to eat bananas. He put me here to bear much fruit, so I could show that I'm a disciple of Jesus. In creation, God created every fruit bearing tree to bear fruit according to its kind. As a follower of Jesus Christ, He has called me to bear fruit in my kind. In John 15, it says He cuts off every branch in Jesus that does not bear fruit and, every branch that does bear fruit, he prunes to be even more fruitful. Our fruit is something that ought to be growing. We ought to be bearing more and more fruit as we mature as Christians, but instead, many Christians are content just to suck the life out of Christians who are producing fruit. That is not what Jesus called us to do. He told us to look at the world through His own lenses and to bear fruit just like He bore fruit. The book of Colossians calls Jesus the "first fruits," and we become the second fruits. This fruit bearing must continue as we reproduce ourselves in others.

Sometimes we get discouraged with our efforts and wonder if any fruit is being born. It may be that we won't see any fruit, but the Bible tells us that our labor in the Lord is not in vain. So we must keep planting seeds. We may not be the one to water them or harvest them, but we will have done what God asked us to do. We have seen the needs and planted seeds for the harvest.

But the fruit of the Spirit is love, joy, peace, forbearance, kindness, goodness, faithfulness, gentleness and self-control. Against such things there is no law.
-Galatians 5:22-23

The greatest proof of Christianity for others is not how far a man can logically analyze his reasons for believing, but how far in practice he will stake his life on his belief.
-T. S. Eliot[79]

---

79 See Appendix: Quote References

12

The Good News

If you wonder if God would ever talk to you or use you in any way, the good news is, yes, He will. We need to listen and be ready. God wants every person He has created to come to Him and ask for forgiveness for his or her sins. Like I did at one time, you might think you are not a sinner because you have not done anything considered as criminal activity. Or maybe you have committed a crime and wonder if God would even consider you for His purposes. The good news again is, yes, He will.

Sin is sin. Whether it is a white lie, murder, theft, cheating, lust—whatever God hates, that is sin. But we must remember that He hates the sin, not the sinner.

In the first book of the Bible, we read that God created the heavens and the earth. Genesis 1:31 tells us that His work was perfect, saying, "God saw all that he had made, and it was very good. And there was evening, and there was morning—the sixth day."

God created a man and woman—Adam and Eve. Genesis describes this creation, stating, "So God created mankind in his own image, in the image of God he created them; male and female he created them" (Genesis 1:27). Since they were made in the image of God, they were able to fellowship with God.

They lived in the Garden of Eden and had no worries for anything because "The LORD God made all kinds of trees grow out of the ground—trees that were pleasing to the eye and good for food. In the middle of the garden were the tree of life and the tree of the knowledge of good and evil" (Genesis 2:9). And God went on to say, "The LORD God took the man and put him in the Garden of Eden to work it and take care of it. And the LORD God commanded the man, 'You are free to eat from any tree in the garden; but you must not eat from the tree of the knowledge of good and evil, for when you eat from it you will certainly die'" (Genesis 2:15-17.)

Satan came to Eve in the form of a serpent and tempted her to eat of the tree of knowledge that God had forbidden them to eat. Then she gave the fruit to Adam, and "through deception and disobedience Adam and Eve sinned against God, causing a break in their relationship with him. Sin is real, and sin is deadly. The guilt that resulted from their disobedience caused Adam and Eve to hide from God and to attempt to cover their personal shame. Because they had disobeyed God's command, they were now flawed and shameful in God's presence."[80]

When reading the section "God's Plan to Save You" in the ESV Daily Reading Bible, God's plan for each of us is made clear. When Adam and Eve were "found" by God when they thought they were hiding (of course, we cannot hide from God), He made the first sacrifice to cover their nakedness. It had never occurred to me before, but God had to kill an animal to make clothing for Adam and Eve.

To have a personal relationship with God, we must come to Him and ask for the forgiveness of our sins. We are separated from God until we do this. The desire to be restored to fellowship with God resides in all of our hearts, and we need the power of God to change our lives. We cannot do this alone or through good works, going to church, donating to charities, or anything else; the only way to complete fellowship is to come to God and ask Him to forgive us. In the section referenced above, The Daily Reading Bible lays this out. In part, it reads:

Why do we need to be saved?
"Truly, truly, I say to you, everyone who commits sin is a slave to sin" (John 8:34.) If we are honest with ourselves, we cannot deny that from the moment of our birth we have done wrong things—things that make us guilty before God and deserving of His judgment. The Bible calls these wrong things sin, and sin separates us from God. And because we are separated from God, we face the awful prospect of "the wrath of God" (John 3:36).
Jesus is the only way
"I am the way, and the truth, and the life. No one comes to the Father except through me" (John 14:6). He did not say that he simply knew the way to heaven; Jesus said he is the only way to heaven. No human effort can give us eternal life. Christ, and Christ alone,

---

[80] ESV The Daily Reading Bible,English Standard Version (ESV), 2006, Good News Publishers (including Crossway Bibles), page 1043

is the one and only Redeemer.
How does Jesus save us?
John the Baptist calls Jesus the "Lamb of God, who takes away the sin of the world" (John 1:29). Jesus came into this world knowing what it would cost him, and he explains that salvation comes through his death on the cross as the perfect and sufficient sacrifice for our sins (John 3:14-15). He bore in his pure being the fullness of sin, that God might forgive sinners and make them pure. And the price of Christ's bearing those sins was death. The gates of salvation are open wide to all who accept his invitation to enter by faith.
Do you believe?
The last verse (John 11:26) actually ends with Jesus asking, "Do you believe this?" It is a question that every person must answer: Do you believe that Jesus Christ is the Son of God? Is Jesus the object of your faith? Not faith in ritual, not faith in sacrifices, not faith in morals, not faith in yourself. Do you believe that Jesus died on the cross to free you from the guilt and judgment of sin? Do you believe that he rose from the grave, breaking the power of death and making a way for you to have eternal life in heaven? If so, you may express your faith in him by praying this prayer:

Heavenly Father, I believe that Jesus Christ is Your Son, and that He died on the cross to save me from my sin. I believe that He rose again to life and that He invites me to live forever with Him in heaven as part of Your family. Because of what Jesus has done, I ask You to forgive me of my sin and give me eternal life. I invite You to come into my heart and life. I want to trust Jesus as my Savior and follow Him as my Lord. Help me to live in a way that pleases and honors You. Amen.[81]

Years ago, after I prayed such a prayer, I wondered what would happen next. I remember feeling wonderful and like I was surrounded by a blanket of love that freed me from everything that had bound me. I asked a trusted friend if I would feel this way forever. Her answer was wise, and I remember it well, "You will feel this way, but it will change. It will deepen and become richer within you and all that you do." To grow in Christ after we have received this blessed gift of salvation is a lifetime event. We must read the Bible, pray, and talk with God daily, remembering to take the time to listen to what God is telling you. We must seek Christian fellowship, following Jesus' example to "Love one another. As I have loved

---

81   Ibid, page 1045

you, so you must love one another" (John 13:34).

There is assurance once we have accepted God's gift. We will continue to sin, for that is our nature. But when this happens, we need to go to God and confess, for Christ died for *all* of our sins. Though we will always have His forgiveness, we must continue to learn how to prevent sins from happening. That task is unique to each of us. I remember hearing someone say, "If you feel far from God, guess who moved?" There may be times we do feel a distance from God, but Jesus our Shepherd will never leaves us alone.

> *My sheep listen to my voice; I know them, and they follow me.*
> *I give them eternal life, and they shall never perish; no one will snatch them out of my hand.*
> *-John 10:27-28*

One last thought before I close this book. Have you ever thought about how much God wants our praise, love, and adoration? Then you might have wondered why God wants us to pray always and praise Him in all we do. Just this year, as I was reading a little book by John Piper, *Life as a Vapor*[82], my question was put to rest. Good advice from our pastor, Kevin Westra, "If you want an answer to anything, look in the Bible."

I cannot quote Piper directly and I encourage you to seek out his book. He explains that in Psalm 96:4 we praise God because He is greatly to be praised. "For great is the Lord and most worthy of praise; He is to be feared above all gods." He is more worthy of praise than anything He has made. In Psalm 147:1, we learn that praise is a pleasure and is an overflowing of our admiration. "Praise the LORD! For it is good to sing praises to our God; for it is pleasant" (Psalm 147:1). And, "In [God's] presence there is fullness of joy; at your right hand are pleasures forevermore" (Psalm 16:11).

God demands supreme praise for our supreme happiness, Piper explains. God does not require our praise to be complete; He knows we won't be complete unless we give Him praise. God's demand for praise is an act of supreme love, not arrogance.

Amen.

---

[82] See Appendix: Suggested Reading and Websites

Appendix 1

Suggested Reading and Websites

Books (Nonfiction)

Angels, (Billy Graham)
Daily Reading Bible, English Standard Version (ESV)
Heaven (Randy Alcorn)
Heaven for Kids (Randy Alcorn)
A Shepherd Looks at Psalm 23 (Phillip Keller)
A Shepherd Looks at the Good Shepherd and His Sheep (Phillip Keller)
66 Love Letters: A Conversation with God that Invites You into His Story (Dr. Larry Crabb)
Life as a Vapor (John Piper)

Websites

www.abecedarian.org/Pages/namesofsatan.htm (names of Satan)
www.biblegateway.com (biblical reference)
www.cochlear.com (hearing loss and *HopeNotes*)
www.epm.org (Randy Alcorn's Eternal Perspectives)
www.inspiredtojournal.net (journal writing)
www.journalinglife.com (journal writing)
www.NMSS.org, MSAA.com (Multiple Sclerosis)
www.scrapbooking.com
www.scrapbooking.about.com
www.creativememories.com (scrapbooking)
www.42explore.com/journl.htm (journal writing)

Appendix 2

Contributor Biographies

Dave Anderson

Dave Anderson specializes in Internet related projects such as Internet marketing and website design. He grew up in northern Iowa but has lived in Minnesota since leaving the Air Force in 1971. He has been married to his very best friend since 1985, and although they don't have any children, they frequently spend time with nieces and nephews as well as their beagle, Bailey, at their lake home in central Minnesota. Dave is an active volunteer for a number of organizations and finds his volunteer work to be very rewarding. He is especially active in the multiple sclerosis family since he has had MS for many years. He has been very blessed to not be severely affected by this mysterious and currently incurable disease. His favorite quotation is from Ralph Waldo Emerson when he said, "It is one of the most beautiful compensations of life, that no man can sincerely try to help another without helping himself."

Rosemary Barkes

Rosemary Barkes won the fourth annual Erma Bombeck Writing Competition in the year 2000, three months after retiring. This unexpected and exhilarating experience propelled her into a writing career. Rosemary is from the small town of Mt. Gilead, Ohio. She worked her way through college twice, as a secretary, waitress, and freelance model. She holds a Bachelor of Science and Bachelor of Arts from the Ohio State University and a Master of Arts from the University of Dayton which she received at age fifty-nine. Her first book, *The Dementia Dance: Maneuvering Through Dementia While Maintaining Your Sanity*, will be published in 2013.

Ben Cachiaras

Ben Cachiaras is Sr. Pastor of Mountain Christian Church in Joppa, Maryland where he lives with his wife, Karla, and three children. His passion is creatively and compellingly sharing the grace and truth of Jesus, and he thinks the most important prayers we can pray are "Help me" and "Disturb me."

Elizabeth Dunkel

Thirteen-year-old Elizabeth Dunkel lives in Dayton, Ohio. Her mother home schools her, along with her two brothers. Among many other things, she enjoys writing, reading, playing the piano, and drawing. Elizabeth aspires to be a published author, and is currently writing a novel. She seeks to honor God and portray the Gospel in all her writing.

Mary Dunkel

Mary Dunkel has happily followed her military husband all over the U.S., but currently lives in Ohio with her family. She is still, by God's grace, home-schooling her three children and thinks it is the best job in the world. In her rare moments of free time, you might find her knitting or sipping a mug of hot tea while reading a good book. She prays her short story will encourage mothers to lean on the Lord for strength through the difficulties and challenges of motherhood.

Linda Fitzpatrick

Linda Fitzpatrick was born in Columbus, Ohio and is one of eight children. She and her siblings were raised in foster homes and later their mother was able to get them back together.

Linda is married to a fine Christian man and has two daughters and four grandchildren. Her husband is retired and they are enjoying their country home. She feels blessed to know both daughters and son-in-laws are Christians.

In her twenties, she started praying that God would make her hungry and thirsty for His Word, and He did just that. In her quest to learn about her Lord, she wanted to help others develop this desire to know God's Word. She started attending Ladies Bible Studies and quickly started leading them. In this journey, she was invited to Bible Study Fellowship. Through BSF, she has learned how to study God's Word and is now a BSF Group Leader.

Vicki Julian

Vicki Julian spent much of her adult life in the corporate world writing grants, guides, and explanatory manuals. She honed her story telling skills as a Sunday school teacher and preschool director. She is the author of *Christmas: A Season for Angels,* Always a Season for Angels, and a contributing author to The Healing Project's *Voices of M.S.* A third book is currently in process. Retired early, Vicki is an M.S. Peer Advocate, Stephen Minister, citizen journalist for *The Humanitarian Examiner,* http://www.examiner.com/humanitarian-in-topeka/vicki-julian, Financial Secretary of the Kansas Authors Club, and remains active in her church while participating in many charitable events.

Christy Kirtlan

Christy Kirtlan has her plate full of fudges and nudges, living in Grove City, Ohio, with her husband of thirteen years, four adult daughters, two sons-in-law, and baby granddaughter. As a pastor's wife, mom, and now grandma, life is very full, hectic, and joyful. Christy enjoys her husband, vacations, and passionately teaching God's Word.

Stan Kirtlan

Stan Kirtlan has been preaching since he was fifteen years old. Growing up in a strong Christian family on a farm in Indiana, a foundation of faith was built in him at a young age. Since leaving the farm for college, Stan has preached in four different churches. The most recent ministry with the Buckeye Christian Church began in 1994. God has "nudged" him through a life that has includes his wife Christy and four beautiful daughters who have grown into young adults and are now starting families of their own. He is enjoying the fun part of family life—grandparenthood!

Julie Lindsey

Julie Shetrone married Steve Lindsey in 1970. They have two children, David Patric, a Yard Master for the CSX Railroad, and Molly, a nurse in the neonatal unit at Mt. Carmel (East) Hospital in Columbus, Ohio. Julie became a librarian because of her interest in so many topics. She loved libraries and reading, so it was natural for her to study Library and Information Science. She is an avid journal keeper finding it comforting to go back and "recapture" some of the events and, possibly, learn from them. When she looks back through her journaling, she can see God had a purpose for her vacillations between Catholicism and Protestantism.

Tamara Payne

Tamara Payne, fifteen at this writing, is eldest of five home schooled siblings. She lives on Ozark Mountain, near the little Mulberry River, in Arkansas. Her hobbies include inductive Bible studies, photography, drawing, writing, reading, singing, and playing the piano. She is amazed that God has given her the ability to put into words what she has in her heart and mind. Tamara is active in her church with Sunday school, Awana, fundraisers, and wherever else she is needed. Her church family supports, guides, and loves her through prayer and constant encouragement. She seeks to continue to grow in God's grace and to be a disciple to the world.

Donna Lee Schillinger

Donna Lee Schillinger lives in rural Arkansas with her husband and two children. She is an award-winning publisher and editor. In 2008, Donna founded On My Own Now Ministries to reach young adults during their transition to independence with biblically-based multimedia events and programs that encourage faith, wise life choices, and Christ-likeness. She is the author of *On My Own Now: Straight Talk from the Proverbs for Young Christian Women who Want to Remain Pure, Debt-free and Regret-free* and editor of a new anthology, *Purity's Big Payoff/Premarital Sex is a Big Rip-off*. Visit her on the Web at www.OnMyOwnNow.com.

Sonja Stauch

Sonja Stauch lives in Grove City, Ohio, with her tiny poodle, Riley. She has a daughter and several grandchildren who fill her life with joy. She is retired from Battelle Memorial Institute where she worked for thirty-five years. Sonja loves making cards and other gifts as a Stampin' Up enthusiast. She loves travel, good movies, music, crocheting, and a good cup of tea shared with friends.

Liz Thompson

Liz Thompson lives in Grove City, Ohio, with her husband, Bob, and wire-haired dachshund, Toby Bear, who is her Certified

Hearing Dog. In 2008, Liz's first book, *Day by Day: The Chronicles of a Hard of Hearing Reporter* was published by Gallaudet University Press. She has a column in *This Week Newspapers(formerly Suburban News Publications - SNP)* in Columbus, Ohio, where she was also a reporter *(SNP)* from 2000-2003. From 2003-2005, she and her husband lived in Arizona where she was a Community Columnist for *The Arizona Republic.* Liz has been a writer for *Hearing Health Magazine* and www.moveoverms.org. She wants to share her faith in God in her writing and pass on the love of writing to the next generation.

Louise Thompson

Louise Thompson, (1918-2007) was a poet, storyteller, and active member of the Linworth United Methodist Church in Columbus, Ohio, from 1940 until shortly prior to her death. She was a loving wife of James Thompson and mother, grandmother, and true friend to many souls during her eighty-nine years. She was active in United Methodist Women for all her adult years. She published several books of poetry and shared her love of the Lord at every opportunity.

Kathleen Grimm Welty

Kathleen Grimm Welty, free-lance writer from Lancaster, Ohio, and has also lived in Illinois and Indiana. She graduated from Taylor University and married Kermit in June, 1973. They have three sons, two daughters-in-law, and five grandchildren. She is a member of Living Hope Free Methodist Church. Kathleen's publishing credits include *Light and Life Magazine*, Kyria digital magazine, Focus on the Family's *Clubhouse Magazine* and *Thriving Family* magazine, ChristianDevotions.us, Evangel (IN), Victoriamag.com, and CBN.com. Previously Kathleen was an artist and assistant for Sunday-school curriculum, magazine lay-out designer, and best of all, a stay-at-home mom. Previously Kathleen was an artist and assistant for Sunday-school curriculum, magazine lay-out designer, and best of all, a stay-at-home mom. After the mommy years, she was an elementary art teacher until 2009. Her life has been solely dedicated for service to Jesus Christ, who is her Lord and Savior. Kathleen prays that her typed words will reflect her love of Christ and her desire that others follow Him, too.

Jan Widman

Jan Widman is a lady who loves Jesus and is particularly

grateful for His unconditional love of her and the forgiveness of her sins. She has been married to Ralph for forty-one years, currently lives in Lynchburg, OH, and calls Mousi and Calico (cats) and Dusti (a strong willed Shi-tzu) family. While Jan's body is disabled from her nursing career, her brain is still a fertile and creative place. She enjoys writing poetry and short essays, sewing, rubber stamping for card making, and most domestic arts (except housework!). Piano playing, reading, and aviation-related topics are of great interest to her. She is the co-pilot, navigator, and cookie baker for the Piper Colt they own and fly. Jan says, "I hope my poetry will bless and 'hit the spot' for you, dear reader."

Carol Wimmer

Carol Wimmer served as a director of music, theatre, and fine arts within three churches from 1976-1998 during which time she wrote many original songs and scripts. Wimmer's ministry began taking an unexpected turn in 1998 when she was given insight into the visible spectrum of light and its connection to the Genesis account of creation. These inspired understandings changed her focus in ministry to full time research. Presently a member of the Society of Biblical Literature and the American Academy of Religion, Carol is pioneering a theology of forward momentum based on light, color and the images of nature. She can be found at www.prismatictheology.com.

Appendix 3

Fudge Recipes

My Grandmother Page and my mother, Mary Day, both made this recipe for hot fudge sauce. The sweet chocolate would bubble in the saucepan, emitting an aroma unsurpassed. The smell and taste of this sauce is one of my favorite childhood memories. Enjoy!

Kaki's Hot Fudge Sauce
    1/4 cup cocoa
    1/2 cup granulated sugar
    1/4 cup milk
    1/4 cup butter
    1 teaspoon vanilla

Mix cocoa and sugar together in saucepan. Heat pan on medium heat while adding the milk and butter. Stir constantly, or as my grandmother's recipe read, "Beat!" Make sure it's mixed well and any lumps are smoothed out. Heat to boiling, and continue to stir (or beat, if you wish). Boil while stirring until the mixture thickens slightly. Remove from heat, add vanilla, and stir. As this mixture cools, it thickens. Pour over ice cream or frozen yogurt, and enjoy. It will harden deliciously on the cold ice cream.

Fudge
    2 cups sugar
    2 tablespoons cocoa
    1/8 tsp cream of tartar
    2/3 cup milk
    1 teaspoon vanilla
    2 tablespoons butter

Mix sugar, cocoa, milk, and cream of tartar, and boil slowly. Stir until ingredients are well blended. Boil to soft ball (238 degrees Fahrenheit). Remove from stove and add butter, but do not stir in. When lukewarm, add vanilla, and beat until it creams, until the shiny appearance disappears and fudge holds shape when dropped from spoon. Spread in buttered pan and cool.

Fantasy Fudge
(www.cooks.com)
    3 cups sugar
    3/4 cup margarine
    2/3 cup undiluted Carnation Evaporated milk
    1 12-ounce package semisweet chocolate pieces
    2 cups Kraft Marshmallow Crème
    1 cup chopped nuts
    1 teaspoon vanilla

Combine sugar, margarine, and milk in heavy 2 1/2 quart saucepan; bring to full rolling boil, stirring constantly. Continue boiling five minutes over medium heat, stirring constantly to prevent scorching. Remove from heat; stir in chocolate pieces until melted. Add marshmallow crème, nuts, and vanilla; beat until well blended. Pour into greased 13x9-inch pan. Cool at room temperature; cut into squares. Makes approximately 3 pounds.

Million Dollar Fudge
(Kathleen Welty[83])
    4 ½ cups sugar
    1 14-oz can evaporated milk
    Boil together for six minutes, stirring constantly.
    Place these ingredients in another bowl:
    2 8-oz Hershey bars, broken into small pieces
    1 12-oz package chocolate chips
    1 pt marshmallow crème
    1 cup walnut pieces

Pour boiled mixture into bowl, mix quickly, pour into 9 x 13

---

[83] This is the recipe I got from my mom. Later, I looked it up on cooks.com and found that they have 101 versions of this same recipe! I suppose some of them are identical, but the six or eight that I read had small variations. I typed the recipe as my mother gave it to me over the phone, but I also included a paragraph from one of the on-line recipes.

buttered pan. Mix sugar and evaporated milk in large saucepan. Bring to boil and boil gently for six minutes. Meanwhile, break Hershey bars into large heat resistant bowl. Add chocolate chips, marshmallow crème, and nuts. Pour boiling mixture over mixture in bowl. Mix quickly and spread in buttered 9 x 13 inch pan. When set, cut into squares.

MAC Fudge
(Mary Ann Carter)

2 1/2 cups sugar
1 stick of real butter (no substitutes)
2/3 cup Half-n-Half (no substitutes)

Stir in saucepan, bring to a boil, and simmer for five minutes. Remove from burner and add:

12 oz semi sweet chocolate chips
pecans or nuts of your choice (any amount you like)
10 oz jar marshmallow cream
Stir together and pour into a 9 x 13 buttered dish and let cool.

Scripture Cake
No one knows where or when this cake was invented. It may have come from Europe, or it may have been created on the Eastern Shore of early North America. It was sweet to eat, and a chance to modestly exhibit knowledge of the Bible. It was fun in the form of an early trivia game, and a great dish to take to a church supper.

As women moved westward across America, the recipe went with them as a small, treasured bit from "back home." It usually traveled along as part of a prized collection of recipes.

The historical cake can still be made today. To play the game as our grandmothers might have played it, read the Biblical list of ingredients and write down your knowledge (or best guess) of the scriptural ingredients. Then, to be on the safe side, look in a King James version of the Bible to verify your answers. You are now ready to make the cake and do your share in continuing a historical, friendly tradition.

To double-check your Biblical baking ingredients, a second, more conventional recipe is listed below the Scripture version. Good luck, and good eating. [84]

---

[84]   http://www.abetterhope.com/funpage.html

Appendix 3: Fudge Recipes

SCRIPTURE CAKE
1½ cups Judges 5:25
3 cups Jeremiah 6:20
6 Jeremiah 17:11
3½ cups Exodus 29:2
2 teaspoons Amos 4:5
2 Chronicles 9:9 to taste
A pinch of Mark 9:50
1 cup Genesis 24:17
1 tablespoon 1 Samuel 14:25
2 cups 1 Samuel 30:12
2 cups chopped dried Song of Solomon 2:13
2 cups slivered or chopped Numbers 17:8

(TRADITIONAL RECIPE)
1½ cups butter
3 cups sugar
6 eggs
3½ cups flower
2 teaspoons baking power
½ teaspoon ground nutmeg
1 teaspoon ground cloves
2 teaspoons cinnamon
1 teaspoon allspice
A pinch of salt
1 cup water
1 tablespoon honey
2 cups raisins
2 cups chopped dried figs
2 cups slivered or chopped almonds
Preheat oven to 325 degrees.

Cream together butter and sugar; beat in eggs one at a time, beating well after each one. Sift together flour, baking powder, salt, and spices. Add alternately with water to creamed mixture.

Stir in honey, fold in raisins, figs, and almonds. Mix well. Turn into two well greased 9x5x3 inch loaf pans. Bake about 60 minutes, making sure not to over bake, until loaves test done by the toothpick test. Let cool for 30 minutes in pans before turning out onto rack.

Appendix 4

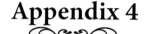

Quote references

Erma Bombeck, (1927-1996)
    For three decades, she chronicled life's absurdities in a syndicated column carried by hundreds of newspapers. She was born Erma Louise Fiste in Dayton, Ohio, to a father who was a city crane operator. At age fifteen, she was hired by the Dayton Herald as a copygirl. Shirley Temple came to Dayton premiering her latest movie. Erma interviewed her, and the story was published on the feature page. That day marked the beginning of her writing career. After college, she began writing a column resulting in syndication appearing in thirty-eight papers the first year. Five years later, her column "At Wit's End" was regular in five hundred and at the time of her death eight hundred newspapers. She authored a number of books.[85]

Benjamin J. Elger
    I could find no information about Benjamin J. Elger to pass on.

T.S. Eliot, (1888-1965)
    T.S. Eliot was an author, playwright, and poet and won The Nobel Prize in Literature in 1948. He was born in St. Louis, Missouri, of an old New England family. He was educated at Harvard and did graduate work in philosophy at the Sorbonne, Harvard, and Merton College, Oxford. He settled in England, where he was for a time a schoolmaster, a bank clerk, and eventually literary editor for the publishing house Faber & Faber, of which he later

---

85   Source: findagrave.com

became a director. He founded and, during the seventeen years of its publication (1922-1939), edited the exclusive and influential literary journal Criterion. In 1927, Eliot became a British citizen and, about the same time, entered the Anglican Church.

Richard J. Foster

Richard J. Foster is a Christian theologian and author in the Quaker tradition. His writings speak to a broad Christian audience. He has been a professor at Friends University and pastor of Evangelical Friends churches.

Benjamin Franklin, (1706-1790)

Benjamin Franklin was born in Boston and was the tenth son of soap maker, Josiah Franklin. Franklin became famous for being a scientist, an inventor, a statesman, a printer, a philosopher, a musician, and an economist. Today, we honor Ben Franklin as one of our Founding Fathers and as one of America's greatest citizens.

William Franklin "Billy" Graham, Jr. (born November 7, 1918)

Billy Graham is an American evangelical Christian evangelist. As of April 25, 2010, when he met with Barack Obama, he has been a spiritual adviser to twelve United States presidents going back to Harry S. Truman and is number seven on Gallup's list of admired people for the twentieth century. He is a Southern Baptist. He rose to celebrity status as his sermons were broadcast on radio and television.

Frank Laubach, (1884 – 1970)

Frank Laubach was a Christian Evangelical missionary and mystic known as "The Apostle to the Illiterates."[86]

Clive Staples Lewis (C.S. Lewis) (1898–1963)

C.S. Lewis was one of the intellectual giants of the twentieth century and arguably the most influential Christian writer of his day. His major contributions in literary criticism, children's literature, fantasy literature, and popular theology brought him international renown and acclaim. He wrote more than thirty books, allowing him to reach a vast audience, and his works continue to attract thousands of new readers every year. His most distinguished and popular accomplishments include *The Chronicles of Narnia, Out of the Silent Planet, The Four Loves,*

---

86   Source: wikipedia.org

The Screwtape Letters, and *Mere Christianity*.

Horace Mann, (1796-1859)
Horace Mann was an educator and a statesman who greatly advanced the cause of universal, free, non-sectarian public schools. Mann also advocated temperance, abolition, hospitals for the mentally ill, and women's rights. His preferred cause was education, about which he remarked that while "other reforms are remedial; education is preventative."

Thomas Merton, (1915-1968)
Thomas Merton is arguably the most influential American Catholic author of the twentieth century. His autobiography, *The Seven Storey Mountain*, has sold over one million copies and has been translated into over fifteen languages. He wrote over sixty other books and hundreds of poems and articles on topics ranging from monastic spirituality to civil rights, nonviolence, and the nuclear arms race.

Dwight L. Moody (1837-1899)
D.L. Moody was an American evangelist who founded the Northfield Schools in Massachusetts, Moody Church, and Moody Bible Institute in Chicago.

Henri Jozef Machiel Nouwen (Nouen), (1932-1996)
Henri Nouwen was a Dutch-born Catholic priest and writer who authored forty books on the spiritual life. Nouwen's books are widely read today by Protestants and Catholics alike. *The Wounded Healer, In the Name of Jesus, Clowning in Rome, The Life of the Beloved* and *The Way of the Heart* are just a few of the more widely recognized titles. After nearly two decades of teaching at the Menninger Foundation Clinic in Topeka, Kansas, and at the University of Notre Dame, Yale University, and Harvard University, he went to share his life with mentally handicapped people at the L'Arche community of Daybreak in Toronto, Canada. After a long period of declining energy, which he chronicled in his final book, *Sabbatical Journey*, he died in September 1996 from a sudden heart attack.[87]

John Ortberg
John Ortberg is the Senior Pastor at Menlo Park Presbyterian

---
[87] Source: wikipedia.org

Church, a church in Northern California with campuses in Menlo Park, Mountain View, and San Mateo. He is the author of many books including *If You Want to Walk on Water, You've Got to Get Out of the Boat*, *The Life You've Always Wanted: Spiritual Growth for Ordinary People*, and his latest book, *The Me I Want To Be*.

John Selden, (1584–1654)

John Selden was an English jurist, scholar of England's ancient laws and constitution, and scholar of Jewish law. He was known as a polymath showing true intellectual depth and breadth; John Milton hailed Selden in 1644 as "the chief of learned men reputed in this land."

Robert Lewis Balfour Stevenson, (1850-1894)

Robert Stevenson lived in Edinburgh, Scotland, and was a novelist, poet, and travel writer. Some of his works include *Treasure Island*, *A Child's Garden of Verses*, *Kidnapped*, and *Strange Case of Dr Jekyll and Mr. Hyde*.

Charles Rozell "Chuck" Swindoll (born October 18, 1934)

Chuck Swindoll is an evangelical Christian pastor, author, educator, and radio preacher. He founded Insight for Living, currently headquartered in Plano, Texas, which airs a radio program of the same name on more than 2,000 stations around the world in fifteen languages. He is currently the senior pastor of Stonebriar Community Church, in Frisco, Texas.

George Swinnock, (1627-1673)

George Swinnock was an English puritan and minister.

Joni Eareckson Tada , (1949-)

A diving accident in 1967 left Joni a quadriplegic in a wheelchair. Today, she is an internationally known mouth artist, a talented vocalist, a radio host, an author of seventeen books, and an advocate for disabled persons worldwide.

J. Hudson Taylor, (1832-1905)

J.H. Taylor was an English missionary to China. He founded the China Inland Mission which, at his death, included 205 mission stations with over 800 missionaries, and 125,000 Chinese

Christians.[88]

Edward Teller (1908–2003)

Teller was a Hungarian-born American theoretical physicist, known colloquially as "the father of the hydrogen bomb," even though he did not care for the title.

Mother Teresa, (1910–1997)

Mother Teresa, born Agnes Gonxha Bojaxhiu, was a Catholic nun of Albanian ethnicity and Indian citizenship, who founded the Missionaries of Charity in Calcutta, India, in 1950. For more than forty-five years, she ministered to the poor, sick, orphaned, and dying, while guiding the Missionaries of Charity's expansion, first throughout India and then in other countries. Following her death, she was beatified by Pope John Paul II and given the title Blessed Teresa of Calcutta.

A. W. Tozer(1897-1963)

Tozer, as he was affectionately known during his lifetime, is widely regarded as one of the most perceptive writers in the twentieth century. He served as pastor of Christian & Missionary Alliance churches in Chicago and Toronto and was a popular speaker and prolific author who wrote with biblical insight and prophetic precision.

---

[88] Source: wholesomeword.com

Appendix 5

Music Notes (Pun Intended)

Source: **www.cyberhymnal.org** unless otherwise noted.

Send the Light, 1890
Charles H. Gabriel (1856-1932)

Growing up on an Iowa farm, Gabriel taught himself to play the family's reed organ. He began teaching in singing schools by age 16, and became well known as a teacher and composer. He served as music director at Grace Methodist Episcopal Church, San Francisco, California (1890-2), then moved to Chicago, Illinois. In 1912 he began working with Homer Rodeheaver's publishing company. His edited some 43 song books, 7 men's (Chorus) books, 19 anthem collections, and 23 cantatas.

There's a call comes ringing over the restless wave,
"Send the light! Send the light!"
There are souls to rescue there are souls to save,
Send the light! Send the light!
Refrain:
Send the light, the blessed Gospel light;
Let it shine from shore to shore!
Send the light, the blessed Gospel light;
Let it shine forevermore!
We have heard the Macedonian call today,
"Send the light! Send the light!"
And a golden offering at the cross we lay,
Send the light! Send the light!
Refrain:

Let us pray that grace may everywhere abound,
"Send the light! Send the light!"
And a Christlike spirit everywhere be found,
Send the light! Send the light!
Refrain:
Let us not grow weary in the work of love,
"Send the light! Send the light!"
Let us gather jewels for a crown above,
Send the light! Send the light!
Refrain:

Sunshine in My Soul, 1887
Words by Eliza E. Hewitt (1841-1920)

After graduation from school, Eliza began teaching. However, her career was cut short by a serious spinal problem. She partially recovered, but was an invalid most of her life. She then turned to hymn writing, which ran in the family--her cousin was hymnist Edgar Stites. Eliza lived all her life in Philadelphia, where she was Sunday school superintendent at Northern Home for Friendless Children, and later at the Calvin Presbyterian Church. She was also a regular contributor to Sunday School Helps.

Music by William J. Kirkpatrick (1838-1921)

Son of a schoolteacher and musician, Kirkpatrick grew up in a musical atmosphere. In 1854, he went to Philadelphia, Pennsylvania to study music and learn a trade; he spent over three years as a carpenter. But he was more interested in music than mechanics, devoting all his leisure time to its study. His ambition at the time was to become a violinist.

There is sunshine in my soul today,
More glorious and bright
Than glows in any earthly sky,
For Jesus is my Light.
Refrain:
O there's sunshine, blessed sunshine,
When the peaceful, happy moments roll;
When Jesus shows His smiling face,
There is sunshine in the soul.
There is music in my soul today,
A carol to my King,

And Jesus, listening, can hear
The songs I cannot sing.
Refrain:
There is springtime in my soul today,
For, when the Lord is near,
The dove of peace sings in my heart,
The flowers of grace appear.
Refrain:
There is gladness in my soul today,
And hope and praise and love,
For blessings which He gives me now,
For joys "laid up" above.
Refrain:

Since Jesus Came into My Heart
Author of lyrics for "Since Jesus Came into My Heart."
Rufus Henry McDaniel (1850, near Ripley, Brown County, Ohio-1940, Dayton, Ohio)

McDaniel wrote these words after the death of his son. McDaniel was educated at Parker's Academy in Claremont County, Ohio. He received a preaching license at age 19, and was ordained a minister of the Christian Church in 1873. After serving at various locations in Ohio, including Hamersville, Higginsport, Centerburg, Sugar Creek and Cincinnati, he retired in Dayton, Ohio. He wrote more than 100 hymns during his life.

Author of music for "Since Jesus Came into My Heart."
Charles Hutchinson Gabriel, (1856, Wilton, Iowa-1932, Los Angeles, California)

Growing up on an Iowa farm, Gabriel taught himself to play the family's reed organ. He began teaching in singing schools by age 16, and became well known as a teacher and composer. He served as music director at Grace Methodist Episcopal Church, San Francisco, California (1890-2), then moved to Chicago, Illinois. In 1912, he began working with Homer Rodeheaver's Publishing Company. He edited some 43 songbooks, 7 men's chorus books, 19 anthem collections and 23 cantatas.

What a wonderful change in my life has been wrought
Since Jesus came into my heart!
I have light in my soul for which long I had sought,

Since Jesus came into my heart!
Refrain:
Since Jesus came into my heart,
Since Jesus came into my heart,
Floods of joy o'er my soul
Like the sea billows roll,
Since Jesus came into my heart.
I have ceased from my wandering and going astray,
Since Jesus came into my heart!
And my sins, which were many, are all washed away,
Since Jesus came into my heart!
Refrain:
I'm possessed of a hope that is steadfast and sure,
Since Jesus came into my heart!
And no dark clouds of doubt now my pathway obscure,
Since Jesus came into my heart!
Refrai:
There's a light in the valley of death now for me,
Since Jesus came into my heart!
And the gates of the City beyond I can see,
Since Jesus came into my heart!
Refrain:
I shall go there to dwell in that City, I know,
Since Jesus came into my heart!
And I'm happy, so happy, as onward I go,
Since Jesus came into my heart!
Refrain

The Unclouded Day, circa 1880
Word and Music by Josiah Kelly Alwood, (1828-1909)

Alwood was a circuit riding preacher in the American Midwest, and later an elder in the North Ohio Conference of the United Brethren Church.

O they tell me of a home far beyond the skies,
O they tell me of a home far away;
O they tell me of a home where no storm clouds rise,
O they tell me of an unclouded day.
Refrain:
O the land of cloudless day,
O the land of an unclouded day,
O they tell me of a home where no storm clouds rise,

O they tell me of an unclouded day.
O they tell me of a home where my friends have gone,
O they tell me of that land far away,
Where the tree of life in eternal bloom
Sheds its fragrance through the unclouded day.
Refrain:
O they tell me of a King in His beauty there,
And they tell me that mine eyes shall behold
Where He sits on the throne that is whiter than snow,
In the city that is made of gold.
Refrain:
O they tell me that He smiles on His children there,
And His smile drives their sorrows all away;
And they tell me that no tears ever come again
In that lovely land of unclouded day.
Refrain:

Thy Word
Words and Music by Amy Grant, (1960-   )

In 1982, Amy Grant was the first Contemporary Christian artist to reach platinum status with the release of her album, *Age to Age*, which also secured her a Grammy for Best Pop Gospel Performance. Though Contemporary Christian music was clearly a growing force in the mid-'80s, no artist had yet crossed over to mainstream success. Then came Grant's 1985 album *Unguarded*. Cracking the pop Top 40, earning platinum and winning a Grammy, *Unguarded* was a challenge within her gospel audience for its secular nature but it proved a watershed for the genre. The track "Find A Way" reached both Top 30 pop and Top 10 Adult Contemporary and its video even aired on MTV. Source: amygrant.com

Chorus:
Thy Word is a lamp unto my feet
And a light unto my path.
Thy Word is a lamp unto my feet,
And a light unto my path.
When I feel afraid,
Think I've lost my way,
Still You're there, right beside me.
Nothing will I fear,
As long as You are near.
Please, be near me to the end

Chorus:
Thy Word is a lamp unto my feet
And a light unto my path.
Thy Word is a lamp unto my feet,
And a light unto my path.
I will not forget
Your love for me and yet,
My heart forever is wandering.
Jesus be my guide,
And hold me to Your side,
And I'll love You to the end.
Chorus:
Thy Word is a lamp unto my feet
And a light unto my path.
Thy Word is a lamp unto my feet,
And a light unto my path.
Nothing will I fear,
As long as You are near.
Please be with me 'til the end.
Thy Word is a lamp unto my feet
And a light unto my path.
Thy Word is a lamp unto my feet
And a light unto my path,
And a light unto my path,
You're the Light unto my path!
Thy word is a lamp unto my feet
And a light unto my path.
Thy word is a lamp unto my feet
And a light unto my path.
And a light unto my path.
You're the light unto my path.

Day by Day from the musical Godspell, 1971
Music and Lyrics: Stephen Schwartz
Source: www.stlyrics.com/lyrics/godspell/daybyday.htm

Day by day
Day by day
Oh Dear Lord
Three things I pray
To see thee more clearly
Love thee more dearly
Follow thee more nearly

Day by day
Day by day
Day by day
Oh Dear Lord
Three things I pray
To see thee more clearly
Love thee more dearly
Follow thee more nearly
Day by day

His Eye is on the Sparrow, 1905
Civilla D. Martin, (1866-1948) Born in Jordan, Nova Scotia, Canada. Died in Atlanta, Georgia
Copyright: Public Domain
Scripture: Matthew 10:29-31

Why should I feel discouraged, why should the shadows come,
Why should my heart be lonely, and long for heav'n and home,
When Jesus is my portion? My constant Friend is He:
His eye is on the sparrow, and I know He watches me;
His eye is on the sparrow, and I know He watches me.
Refrain:
I sing because I'm happy, I sing because I'm free,
For His eye is on the sparrow, and I know He watches me.
"Let not your heart be troubled," His tender word I hear,
And resting on His goodness, I lose my doubts and fears;
Though by the path He leadeth, but one step I may see;
His eye is on the sparrow, and I know He watches me;
His eye is on the sparrow, and I know He watches me.
Whenever I am tempted, whenever clouds arise,
When songs give place to sighing, when hope within me dies,
I draw the closer to Him, from care He sets me free;
His eye is on the sparrow, and I know He watches me;
His eye is on the sparrow, and I know He watches me.

This Little Light of Mine
Written by Harry Dixon Loes (1895-1965) in about 1920.

Loes, who studied at the Moody Bible Institute and the American Conservatory of Music, was a musical composer, and teacher, who wrote, and co-wrote, several other gospel songs. The song has since entered the folk tradition, first being collected by John Lomax in 1939. Often thought of as a Negro spiritual, it does not, however, appear in any collection of jubilee or plantation songs from the nineteenth century:

>This little light of mine, I'm gonna let it shine.
>This little light of mine, I'm gonna let it shine, let it shine, let it shine, let it shine.
>Won't let Satan blow it out.
>I'm gonna let it shine.
>Won't let Satan blow it out.
>I'm gonna let it shine, let it shine, let it shine, let it shine.
>Let it shine 'til Jesus comes.
>I'm gonna let it shine.
>Let it shine 'til Jesus comes.
>I'm gonna let it shine, let it shine, let it shine, let it shine.
>Hide it under a bushel - NO!
>I'm gonna let it shine.
>Hide it under a bushel - NO!
>I'm gonna let it shine, Let it shine, let it shine, let it shine.
>Let it shine over the whole wide world,
>I'm gonna let it shine.
>Let it shine over the whole wide world,
>I'm gonna let it shine, let it shine, let it shine, let it shine.

When We See Christ
Words and music by Esther Kerr Rusthoi (1909-1962)

>(1) Oft times the day seems long, our trials hard to bear,
>We're tempted to complain, to murmur and despair;
>But Christ will soon appear to catch His Bride away,
>All tears forever over in God's eternal day.
>**Refrain:**
>It will be worth it all when we see Jesus,
>Life's trials will seem so small when we see Christ;
>One glimpse of His dear face all sorrow will erase,
>So bravely run the race till we see Christ.
>(2) Sometimes the sky looks dark with not a ray of light,
>We're tossed and driven on , no human help in sight;
>But there is one in heav'n who knows our deepest care,
>Let Jesus solve your problem - just go to Him in pray'r.
>**Refrain:**
>It will be worth it all when we see Jesus,
>Life's trials will seem so small when we see Christ;

One glimpse of His dear face all sorrow will erase,
So bravely run the race till we see Christ.
(3) Life's day will soon be o'er, all storms forever past,
We'll cross the great divide, to glory, safe at last;
We'll share the joys of heav'n - a harp, a home, a crown,
The tempter will be banished, we'll lay our burden down.
Refrain:
It will be worth it all when we see Jesus,
Life's trials will seem so small when we see Christ;
One glimpse of His dear face all sorrow will erase,
So bravely run the race till we see Christ.

Have Thine Own Way, Lord
Lyrics by Adelaide A. Pollard, 1907
Music by George C. Stebbins, 1907

Have Thine own way, Lord! Have Thine own way!
Thou art the Potter, I am the clay.
Mold me and make me after Thy will,
While I am waiting, yielded and still.
Have Thine own way, Lord! Have Thine own way!
Search me and try me, Master, today!
Whiter than snow, Lord, wash me just now,
As in Thy presence humbly I bow.
Have Thine own way, Lord! Have Thine own way!
Wounded and weary, help me, I pray!
Power, all power, surely is Thine!
Touch me and heal me, Savior divine.
Have Thine own way, Lord! Have Thine own way!
Hold o'er my being absolute sway!
Fill with Thy Spirit 'till all shall see
Christ only, always, living in me.

Savior Like a Shepherd
Lyricist: attr. Dorothy Ann Thrupp
Lyrics Date: 1836
Composer: William B. Bradbury
Music Date: 1838
Scripture: John 10:14, Psalm 23

Savior, like a shepherd lead us, much we need Thy tender care;
In Thy pleasant pastures feed us, for our use Thy folds prepare.
Blessèd Jesus, blessèd Jesus! Thou hast bought us, Thine we are.

Blessèd Jesus, blessèd Jesus! Thou hast bought us, Thine we are.

We are Thine, Thou dost befriend us, be the guardian of our way;
Keep Thy flock, from sin defend us, seek us when we go astray.
Blessèd Jesus, blessèd Jesus! Hear, O hear us when we pray.
Blessèd Jesus, blessèd Jesus! Hear, O hear us when we pray.

Thou hast promised to receive us, poor and sinful though we be;
Thou hast mercy to relieve us, grace to cleanse and power to free.
Blessèd Jesus, blessèd Jesus! We will early turn to Thee.
Blessèd Jesus, blessèd Jesus! We will early turn to Thee.

Early let us seek Thy favor, early let us do Thy will;
Blessèd Lord and only Savior, with Thy love our bosoms fill.
Blessèd Jesus, blessèd Jesus! Thou hast loved us, love us still.
Blessèd Jesus, blessèd Jesus! Thou hast loved us, love us still.

Made With Love
By Liz Thompson, (1951-),
1991 based on John 10:11-18

The tag upon the worn old quilt said it was made with love.
The sweater that my grandma knit, I know she made with love.
The needles with the thread or yarn spun the gift of love
To keep me warm and comfortable when cold winds blow above.
Chorus 1:
Made with love, made with love; the time it took
amazed me so, I knew they loved me so. Made with love, made
with love -- and think that God loves me even more.
God sent His Son to this old land to help us learn our way.
He used a tough, but gentle hand to lead us through the day.
The voice of the Good Shepherd is like music to our ears
We as his sheep should run to him and let him know we hear!
Chorus 2:
Made with love, made with love. A love I never
knew before, how could he love me so? Made with love, made
with love -- Jesus' love is pure and clear, Jesus' love is always
near. Made with love.
So when you read a tag that say, I am made with love.
Remember Jesus died for you, the greatest gift of all!
Because He died we all can live with him forever more.
Hold out your hands and use your gifts to praise and honor God.

Chorus 3:
Made with love, made with love. He calls with his
sweet, gentle voice you know you must obey. Made with love,
made with love. God made you and me with his love. Let your
life tag read, "Made with love."

The Truth
By Liz Thompson, 1994,
Scripture: John 8:31

We're looking for our freedom, every way we turn
Freedom from anxiety and freedom from all scorn.
Looking, waiting, searching; wanting to be free
When all we really have to do is truly believe.
Chorus:
And the truth will make you free, free to believe
And the truth will make you free, then you'll truly see.
Wandering so lonely, through the highs and lows
Wondering when will the pain finally cease and go.
Hoping for the sunshine, hoping rain will go away
When the rain is a necessity, it mustn't go away.
When the storm is coming, turn on all the lights
Draw from all the power you can and you will see the light.
Storms are so important, they blow away debris
Rain falls and the seeds begin to grow into a tree.
And the truth will make you free, free to believe
And the truth will make you free, then you'll truly see... that
Jesus is our freedom, Jesus is our light.
He is the source of all our power, all our truth and might.
And like the tiny sparrow, he holds us in his hands.
He'll let us fly all through our life but his hands stay open
 wide.
And the truth will make you free, free to believe
And the truth will make you free, then you'll truly see.
Then you will be free.
For Jesus is our freedom.

Breathe on Me Breath of God
Edwin Hatch (1835-1889) Derby, England

Hatch attended Cambridge and Pembroke College, Oxford (BA in honors, 1857). He was ordained an Anglican priest in 1859, then went to Toronto, Canada, where he became a professor of classics at Trinity College. He later became rector of a high school in Quebec. He returned to England in 1867, serving as vice-principal of St. Mary's Hall, Oxford. In 1883, he became rector at Purleigh. A well known scholar, he wrote a concordance to the Septuagint, essays on Biblical Greek, gave Bampton Lectures in 1880, and Hibbert Lectures in 1888.

Robert Jackson (1842-1914) Lancashire, England

Jackson's father played the organ at St. Peter's Church in Oldham. Robert attended the Royal Academy of Music, and served as organist at St. Mark's Church at Grosvenor Square in London. He also played in the Birmingham Symphony Orchestra. In 1868, he took over his father's duties at St. Peter's in Oldham, and played the organ there 46 years (together they served almost an entire century). He also served as head of the Oldham Musical Society, 1891-1906.

Holy, Holy, Holy
Words: Reginald Heber, (1783-1826)

Heber attended Brasenose College, Oxford, where he won a number of awards in English and Latin. He received a fellowship to All Souls College, and later became Rector at Hodnet, Shropshire, England. In 1823, he became, somewhat reluctantly, Bishop of Calcutta, India. Most of his hymns were not published until after his death; 57 of them appeared in Hymns Written and Adapted to the Weekly Church Service of the Year (London: J. Murray, 1827). Heber wrote this hymn for Trinity Sunday while he was Vicar of Hodnet, Shropsire, England.

Music: Nicaea, John B. Dykes, (1823-1876)

At age 12, Dykes became assistant organist at St. John's Church in Hull, where his grandfather was vicar. He studied at Wakefield and St. Catherine's Hall in Cambridge, where he was a Dikes Scholar, President of the Cambridge University Musical Society, and earned a BA in Classics. In 1848, he became curate at Malton, Yorkshire. For a Short time, he was canon of Durham Cathedral, then precentor (1849-1862). In 1862 he became Vicar of St. Oswald's, Durham (he named a son John St. Oswald Dykes, and one of his tunes St. Oswald.) Dykes published sermons and articles on religion, but is best known for composing over 300 hymn tunes. In his music, as in his ecclesiastical work, he was less dogmatic than many of his contemporaries about theological controversies of the day--he often fulfilled requests for tunes for non-Anglican hymns. In addition to his gift for writing music, he played organ, piano, violin, and horn.

>Holy, holy, holy! Lord God Almighty!
>Early in the morning our song shall rise to Thee;
>Holy, holy, holy, merciful and mighty!
>God in three Persons, blessed Trinity!
>Holy, holy, holy! All the saints adore Thee,
>Casting down their golden crowns around the glassy sea;
>Cherubim and seraphim falling down before Thee,
>Who was, and is, and evermore shall be.
>Holy, holy, holy! though the darkness hide Thee,
>Though the eye of sinful man Thy glory may not see;
>Only Thou art holy; there is none beside Thee,
>Perfect in power, in love, and purity.
>Holy, holy, holy! Lord God Almighty!
>All Thy works shall praise Thy Name, in earth, and sky, and sea;
>Holy, holy, holy; merciful and mighty!
>God in three Persons, blessed Trinity!

Come Thou Fount of Every Blessing, 1758
Words by Robert Robinson (1735-1790)
Music by John Wyeth (1770-1858)

Robinson's widowed mother sent him at age 14 to London, to learn the trade of barber and hair dresser. However, his master found he enjoyed reading more than work. Converted to Christ at age 17, Robinson became a Methodist minister. He later moved to the Baptist church and pastored in Cambridge, England. He wrote a number of hymns, as well as on the subject of theology. His later life was evidently not an easy one, judging from a well known story about his hymn "Come, thou Found of Every Blessing." One day, he encountered a woman who was studying a hymnal, and she asked how he liked the hymn she was humming. In tears, he replied, "Madam, I am the poor unhappy man who wrote that hymn many years ago, and I would give a thousand worlds, if I had them, to enjoy the feelings I had then.

As a boy, Wyeth was apprenticed to a printer. At age 21, he became the manager of a printing company in Santo Domingo, only to barely escape with his life in the insurrection there. In 1792, he returned to America and settled in Harrisburg, Pennsylvania, where he became involved in the publishing business and co-owned a newspaper (The Oracle of Dauphin). After only a year in Harrisburg, President George Washington appointed him postmaster; he lost his office five years later when President John Adams declared the position to be incompatible with involvement in newspapers.

> Come, Thou Fount of every blessing,
> Tune my heart to sing Thy grace;
> Streams of mercy, never ceasing,
> Call for songs of loudest praise.
> Teach me some melodious sonnet,
> Sung by flaming tongues above.
> Praise the mount! I'm fixed upon it,
> Mount of Thy redeeming love.
> Sorrowing I shall be in spirit,
> Till released from flesh and sin,
> Yet from what I do inherit,
> Here Thy praises I'll begin;
> Here I raise my Ebenezer;
> Here by Thy great help I've come;
> And I hope, by Thy good pleasure,
> Safely to arrive at home.
> Jesus sought me when a stranger,
> Wandering from the fold of God;
> He, to rescue me from danger,
> Interposed His precious blood;
> How His kindness yet pursues me
> Mortal tongue can never tell,
> Clothed in flesh, till death shall loose me
> I cannot proclaim it well.
> O to grace how great a debtor
> Daily I'm constrained to be!
> Let Thy goodness, like a fetter,
> Bind my wandering heart to Thee.
> Prone to wander, Lord, I feel it,
> Prone to leave the God I love;
> Here's my heart, O take and seal it,
> Seal it for Thy courts above.
> O that day when freed from sinning,
> I shall see Thy lovely face;
> Clothed then in blood washed linen

How I'll sing Thy sovereign grace;
Come, my Lord, no longer tarry,
Take my ransomed soul away;
Send thine angels now to carry
Me to realms of endless day.

CPSIA information can be obtained at www.ICGtesting.com
Printed in the USA
BVOW030446101012

302154BV00013B/1/P